Rodale's Treasury of Christmas Crafts

Holiday Welcome Wreaths

Rodale's Treasury of Christmas Crafts

Holiday Welcome Wreaths

Rodale Press, Emmaus, Pennsylvania

Our Mission
We publish books that empower people's lives.

RODALE BOOKS

Rodale Press Staff

Executive Editor
Margaret Lydic Balitas

Copy Editor
Carolyn R. Mandarano

Editor
Karen Bolesta

Book Designer
Patricia Field

Cover Photographer
Mitch Mandel

If you have any questions or comments concerning this book, please write to:

Rodale Press, Inc.
Book Readers' Service
33 East Minor Street
Emmaus, PA 18098

Printed in the United States of America
Published by Rodale Press, Inc.
Distributed in the book trade by St. Martin's Press.

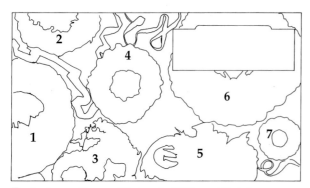

Projects on Cover: (1) Apple Village Christmas, (2) Woodland Christmas Bounty, (3) Lacy and Lovely Heart Wreath, (4) Cinnamon Santas, (5) Grand English Bow Wreath, (6) Holiday Symphony and (7) Visions of Sugarplums

For Chapelle Ltd.
Owner
Jo Packham

Staff
Trice Boerens
Gaylene Byers
Holly Fuller
Cherie Hanson
Susan Jorgensen
Margaret Shields Marti

Jackie McCowen
Barbara Milburn
Pamela Randall
Jennifer Roberts
Florence Stacey
Nancy Whitley

Photography
Ryne Hazen, Gary Rohman

Book Design, Project Design and Text
Chapelle Ltd., Ogden, Utah 84401 © 1993 by Chapelle Ltd.

The author and editors who compiled this book have tried to make all of the contents as accurate and as correct as possible. Graphs, illustrations, photographs and text have all been carefully checked and cross-checked. However, due to the variability of local conditions, tools and supplies, personal skill and so on, Rodale Press assumes no responsibility for any injuries suffered or for damages or other losses incurred that result from the material presented herein. All instructions should be carefully studied and clearly understood before beginning a project.

Library of Congress Cataloging-in-Publication Data

Holiday welcome wreaths.
    p. cm. -- (Rodale's treasury of Christmas crafts)
    ISBN 0–87596–601–2 hardcover
    1. Wreaths. 2. Holiday decorations. I. Rodale Press.
II. Series.
TT899 . 75 . H64   1993
745 . 594 ' 1--dc20   93–29728
                                                      CIP

$\mathcal{C}$ontents

Silvery Branches

Frosted pinecones, gleaming branches and red berries combine for a crisp, contemporary look.

MATERIALS

About thirty 12"–15"-long twigs
Spray paints: pewter, white
Craft wire
Needlenose pliers
Wire cutters
Hot glue gun and glue sticks
About one hundred ten 6"–8"-long sprigs of
  preserved juniper
Twenty sprigs of dried red berries
Seventeen small pinecones
Acrylic paint: pearlescent*
Sponge

*See "Suppliers" on page 128.

DIRECTIONS

1. Spray paint twigs completely with pewter, turning to cover all sides. Allow to dry.

2. To make wreath base, select five of the thickest, sturdiest twigs. Place on flat surface, overlapping ends by 1" to 2". Cut twenty-five 5" lengths of wire. Bind twigs together where they overlap. Using needlenose pliers, twist ends of wire bindings into neat, tight knots; trim excess wire close to knots. Arrange second layer of twigs over first and wire layers together. Continue to wire twigs together, keeping inside edge even and allowing twig ends to extend at varying lengths from outside edge. Spray paint entire wreath lightly with pewter to cover wire. Allow to dry.

3. Glue juniper sprigs to top surface of twig base, with tops of sprigs pointing in same direction. Overlap sprigs slightly. Glue berry sprigs among juniper sprigs as desired.

4. Spray paint pinecones with white. Allow to dry. Sponge-paint pinecones with pearlescent. Allow to dry. Glue pinecones to base among juniper sprigs; see photo for placement.

5. For hanger, cut one 6" length of craft wire. Wrap ends around a thick twig at top back of wreath.

A Golden Christmas

This elegant gilded swag will reflect the warm shimmer of Christmas lights and candles in your home.

MATERIALS

6'-long artificial pine bough swag
Spray paint: metallic gold
Seven 1¼"-tall straw baskets
Six 1"-tall wire baskets
Assorted small pinecones
Four wooden spools
Three 2"-diameter straw wreaths
Two 1¼"-diameter craft bird's nests
Assorted wooden beads
Eighteen assorted dried fruits: apple slices, orange slices, lime slices, kiwi slices, small pomegranates*
Twelve dried pea pods
Seventeen sprigs of dried pepper berries
Sixty large whole bay leaves
Hot glue gun and glue sticks

*See "General Instructions" on page 126 for drying your own fruit.

DIRECTIONS

1. Lay swag on flat, protected surface. Spray very lightly with metallic gold. Allow to dry.

2. Spray baskets, pinecones, spools, wreaths, bird's nests, beads, dried fruits, pea pods, pepper berries and bay leaves lightly with metallic gold. Allow all to dry.

3. Glue items to swag as desired; see photo for ideas.

Try This

Spray the swag with silver, blue or white paint to match your holiday decor. To make the swag decorations easily changeable, attach them with craft wire or thread.

Sew Very Merry

Create this unique wreath for a friend or relative who loves to sew. It will be cherished year-round!

MATERIALS

12"-diameter Styrofoam base
Scraps of cream fabric
Scraps of brocade fabric
Scraps of sheer white fabric
Scraps of ecru and cream crochet and lace
Straight pins with large heads
Regular straight pins
Hot glue gun and glue sticks
One pair of rimless doll glasses
One pair of embroidery scissors
Three 1¼"-long wooden spools
Four ¾"-long wooden spools
Embroidery floss: pale pink, light blue, ivory, white
One package of white seed beads*
Embroidery needle
Three velvet leaves
Assorted old buttons
Assorted sewing notions: snaps, papers of needles, miniature pincushion, thimbles, needle threaders
Assorted charms: miniature scissors, heart, miniature clothespin
6" length of ¼"-wide cream polyester ribbon

*See "Suppliers" on page 128.

DIRECTIONS

1. Experiment with covering base using fabric, crochet and lace scraps. Use large-headed straight pins on back of wreath to pin items in place until arrangement is satisfactory. Glue, if desired, or leave pins in place so fabric may be easily removed from base.

2. Wrap each 1¼"-long spool in one color of embroidery floss, leaving 6"–7"-long tail of floss. Repeat with ¾"-long spools. Glue spools to base; see photo for placement. Attach doll glasses, scissors, buttons, velvet leaves, sewing notions and charms to base as desired; see photo for ideas. Use glue directly on item, or glue regular straight pin to back of item and insert pin in base. Loop tails of floss from spools over wreath as desired, gluing where needed.

3. Thread embroidery needle with white floss; do not cut or knot floss. String seed beads on floss loosely so string bends easily. Cut and knot floss at skein end of bead string. Sew opposite end where desired to fabric-covered base; secure. Loop bead string as desired on base over and under other items, gluing as needed to secure. Insert eight to ten regular straight pins in pincushion.

4. To make hanger, loop polyester ribbon and knot ends. Glue knot to back of wreath.

pple Rose Arch

Hang this lovely arch above a door or window for a touch of cheerful color.

MATERIALS

26"-long grapevine arch
Two 16-ounce packages of golden delicious
   apple chips*
Twelve narrow rubber bands
Spray bottle of water
Cookie sheet
One twelve-cup muffin tin
Twelve yellow artificial stamen groupings
Hot glue gun and glue sticks
5 yards of pale yellow sheer polyester ribbon
Twenty-four velvet geranium leaves
One large bunch of red canella berries
   (available at florist-supply stores)
Thread

*See "General Instructions" on page 126 for
drying your own apple chips.

DIRECTIONS

1. To make apple roses, preheat oven to 150°F.
Spread contents of one package of apple chips
on cookie sheet. Spray lightly with water.
Place in oven for 3–4 minutes. Turn chips.
Spray again and heat 2–3 minutes more. Shape
flowers quickly, while chips are as warm as
possible. Using three to four chips for each
rose, wrap first chip tightly for center, adding
new layers in progressively looser wraps.

Hold chips tightly together at bottom while
shaping. Curl outer petals back slightly for
open rose effect; curl more tightly for bud
effect. Secure each rose bottom with a tightly
wrapped rubber band. Place bottom down in
muffin tin to cool completely. If chips dry out
before shaping is completed, spray again and
return to oven for 2–3 minutes. Repeat with
remaining chips to make twelve roses.

2. Remove rubber bands from cooled, dry
roses. Glue one flower center in center of
each rose.

3. To make bow, gather ribbon into twenty-
two 1¼"–3"-long loops at center, leaving 15"-
long tail on one end and 14"-long tail on
opposite end. Wrap loops with thread ½"
from bottom; secure.

4. Glue bottom of bow to arch at right of top
center. Twisting ribbon slightly, weave tails
through grapevine, gluing as needed to
secure. Notch ribbon tails.

5. Beginning at top center, glue apple roses
to arch as desired; see photo for ideas. Glue
geranium leaves to arch, clustering most
leaves at top center around roses. Divide
canella berry bunch into single berries and
clusters of two to four. Glue to arch among
roses and geranium leaves; see photo.

Evergreen Candy Cane

Create a delightful holiday decoration, sparkling with tiny lights!

MATERIALS

30"-tall cane-shaped wire base
Thirty bunches of eight 7"–9"-long fresh or
  artificial pine boughs
Florist's wire
Wire cutters
Florist's tape
Two 25'-long strings of miniature red
  and white lights
6 yards of 2"-wide red wired ribbon

DIRECTIONS

1. For hanger, cut one 14" length of florist's
wire. Double to make one 7" length. Make
loop and twist ends securely around wire base
at top of candy cane.

2. From florist's wire, cut twenty-five 6"
lengths. Wrap end of one bunch of boughs
with florist's wire. Cover wired end with
florist's tape. Repeat with twenty-four additional bunches of boughs. Leave remaining
boughs unwired.

3. Beginning at top of base, secure bunched
pine boughs to frame with florist's wire,
slightly overlapping previous bunches to
cover wired ends. Fill in gaps with remaining
pine boughs as needed. Fan out boughs to
cover edges of base.

4. To make bow, fold ribbon into 10"-long
loops, leaving 14"-long tails; see Diagram 1.
Handling loops as one, fold in center. Wrap
with florist's wire 2" from bottom of fold; see
Diagram 2. Fluff bow. Wire bow to wreath,
nestling bow bottom into pine boughs to hide
wire wrapping; see photo for placement.
Notch bow tails.

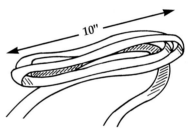

Diagram 1

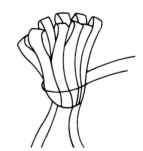

Diagram 2

5. Beginning at bottom of wreath, attach lights
by weaving cords through and around pine
boughs. If using fresh pine boughs, remove
lights as soon as boughs begin to dry out.

$\mathcal{V}$isions of Sugarplums

Tempting candies in holiday hues bring a Christmas Eve vision to life!

MATERIALS

7"-diameter, flat or rounded Styrofoam base
3 yards of 1½"-wide green craft ribbon
Tacky glue
Straight pins
12" length of ⅛"-wide green ribbon
1½ pounds of assorted red, green and white
   hard candies, ribbon candy, jelly beans
   and gumdrops
Hot glue gun and glue sticks

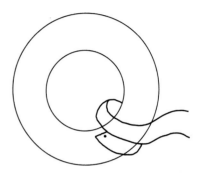

Diagram

DIRECTIONS

1. Using tacky glue, glue one end of craft ribbon to base; secure with straight pin. Allow glue to dry. Wrap craft ribbon around base, overlapping edges by ½" and gluing as needed; see diagram. Secure with pins until glue dries. Remove pins.

2. To make hanger, loop ⅛"-wide ribbon around base, matching ends. Knot ribbon close to base, then knot ribbon ends, making a loop.

3. Hot-glue largest candies to base first, spacing them 1½" to 2" apart. Fill in with medium-size candies, then small candies, covering inside and outside edges of base.

Red-Hot Holiday

This bright wreath will add south-of-the-border spice to your festivities.

MATERIALS

10"-diameter wire base
Thirty-three dozen 2"–2½"-long red
  chili peppers
Ball of jute
Hot glue gun and glue sticks
Four to five sprigs of preserved cedar
Five to six sprigs of dried berries
Five pearl onions
Plastic gloves

DIRECTIONS

1. Purchase dried peppers, or dry your own by hanging in a cool room until skins shrivel and seeds shake freely inside each pepper. Wear plastic gloves when working with peppers. Do not rub eyes, nose or mouth after handling peppers; wash hands thoroughly with soap and water. Keep out of reach of children and pets.

2. Cut fifty 12" lengths of jute. Tie dried peppers securely in bundles of five or six by wrapping jute around stems, leaving jute tails hanging free. Reserve remaining peppers. Tie bundles to base using jute tails. Knot tails and secure to base with glue. Fan out bundles to cover base; see photo. Fill in gaps by gluing reserved peppers between tied bundles.

3. For hanger, cut desired length of jute. Loop and tie to base at top of wreath.

4. Glue cedar sprigs to bottom center of wreath in a fan shape. Glue berry sprigs as desired over cedar sprigs. Cluster pearl onions on bottom center of base, covering ends of cedar sprigs and berry sprigs; see photo.

oodland Home

This charming country wreath lends warmth to your home year-round.

MATERIALS

24"-diameter grapevine base
Sixty 8"-long fresh or artificial pine boughs
Florist's tape
Florist's wire
Wire cutters
Hot glue gun and glue sticks
Five assorted craft bird's nests
Nine ½"-long craft bird eggs
Six 1"-long craft bird eggs
Dried whole artichokes and pomegranates
   (available at florist-supply stores)
Three to four large nuts
Assorted pinecones
Holly leaves
Two to three sweet gum seed capsules*
Three plastic apples
Acrylic paints: red, brown
Paintbrush

*Other types of prickly seed pods may
be substituted.

DIRECTIONS

1. Tape forty pine boughs together in fan-shaped groups of five. Leave twenty boughs untaped. Wire pine bough fans to base, beginning at top and working down right and left curves. Overlap fans slightly to cover tape and wire.

2. Glue two bird's nests to base at bottom left. Glue three bird's nests to base at right, partway up curve. Glue three bird eggs in center of each nest, placing smaller eggs in smaller nests and larger eggs in larger nests. Glue dried pomegranates, nuts, pinecones and holly leaves around bird's nests as desired; see photo for ideas. Paint apples red and stems brown. Allow to dry. Glue apples, artichokes and seed capsules to base as desired.

3. Glue loose pine boughs to base, trimming as needed to fill in around nests, pinecones, artichokes, nuts, apples and seed capsules.

4. To make hanger, cut one 14" length of florist's wire. Double to make one 7" length. Loop doubled wire and twist tails around grapevine at top back of wreath.

Christmas Nest

Let this pretty bird winter at your home in her Christmas tree nest!

MATERIALS

25"-tall Christmas tree–shaped wire base
7"-long scrap of split pine or fir with bark
   (available from a Christmas tree dealer or
   wood lot)
Sixty bunches of eight 7"–9"-long fresh or
   artificial pine boughs
Drill with ⅛" bit
Florist's wire
Wire cutters
Florist's tape
Eight 1½"-long wooden acorns
Acrylic paints: dark brown, light brown
Paintbrush
Sponge
Acrylic matte-finish spray
Hot glue gun and glue sticks
Thirty pinecones
Twelve sprigs of dried berries
One 3½"-long wooden bird
Miniature berry wreath to fit around
   bird's neck
3"-diameter craft bird's nest
Three 7"–8"-long twigs

DIRECTIONS

1. To make trunk, drill two holes through split
pine or fir scrap near top end. Using florist's
wire, secure scrap, bark side up, to center bottom of base by looping wire through drilled
holes and base; see diagram and photo.

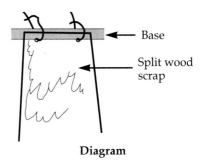

Diagram

2. From florist's wire, cut fifty 6" lengths. Wrap
end of one pine bough bunch with one piece
of wire. Wrap wire with florist's tape. Repeat
with forty-nine additional pine bough bunches. Leave remaining bunches unwired to use
as filler.

3. Secure wired end of one bunch to base with
short length of florist's wire, fanning out individual boughs. Repeat with remaining wired
bunches. Fill in gaps by wiring remaining pine
boughs to base.

4. Drill hole through each wooden acorn just
below acorn cap. Paint acorn bottoms light
brown. Allow to dry. Paint acorn caps dark
brown. Allow to dry. Coat with matte-finish
spray. Cut eight 8" lengths of florist's wire.
Pass one length of wire through hole in each
acorn; set aside.

5. Paint wooden bird light brown. Allow to
dry. Using sponge, add feather markings in
dark brown. Allow to dry. Coat with matte-

finish spray. Glue miniature berry wreath around bird's neck. Glue one berry sprig to beak.

6. Glue one edge of bird's nest to pine boughs right of tree bottom center. Glue bird to edge of nest, resting against pine boughs; see photo on page 22. Glue twigs under nest as if supporting it. Cluster pinecones around bird's nest as desired. Make two smaller clusters of pinecones left of center and third cluster of two pinecones slightly above bird's nest. Wire acorns to boughs among pinecones as desired. Glue remainder of berry sprigs among pinecones as desired; see photo for ideas.

7. To make hanger, cut one 14" length of florist's wire. Double to make one 7" length. Make loop and twist wire ends around base slightly below top of tree at back.

Try This

Pine boughs may be lightly sprayed with silver or gold paint before adding bird, nest, pinecones, acorns and berries. Allow boughs to dry before gluing on other items.

Miniatures, such as squirrels and other tree-dwelling creatures, may be purchased at craft stores, painted and added to your wreath.

Opposite: Cinnamon Santas

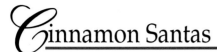innamon Santas

Sprightly cinnamon stick Santas add Christmas color to this wreath. (Project pictured on previous page.)

MATERIALS

11"-diameter grapevine base
Spray paint: brown
8" length of ¼"-wide red polyester ribbon
Forty-eight whole cinnamon sticks
Acrylic paints: red, white, tan, black
Paintbrushes
Straight pin
2½ yards of ¾"-wide red wired ribbon;
   matching thread
Eighty assorted pinecones
Sixteen sweet gum seed capsules
Twenty buckeye seed pods*
Dried orange slices, pea pods, cranberries,
   small pomegranates**
Hot glue gun and glue sticks

*Other prickly seed pods may be substituted.
**See "General Instructions" on page 126 for drying your own orange slices, pea pods, cranberries and pomegranates.

DIRECTIONS

1. Spray paint base brown. Allow to dry.

2. To make hanger, loop polyester ribbon and tie to base.

3. For Santas, paint sixteen cinnamon sticks according to Diagram 1. Allow to dry. Dip head of straight pin in black paint; dab two eyes on each Santa face. For pom-pom, paint a white dot on side of each Santa hat. Allow to dry.

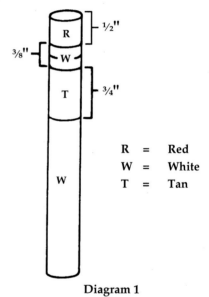

R = Red
W = White
T = Tan

Diagram 1

4. From red wired ribbon, cut twenty-four 3¾" lengths to make miniature bows. Fold each length into three equal loops; see Diagram 2A. Fold loops in half; see Diagram 2B. Sew through bottom of folds to secure. Fluff bows.

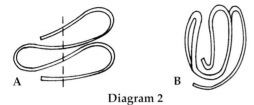

Diagram 2

5. To cover a 4" section of base, experiment with different arrangements, using ten pinecones, two cinnamon Santas, three or four unpainted cinnamon sticks, two sweet gum seed capsules, one or two dried orange slices, one or two pea pods, three bows and other assorted dried items as desired. Glue items in place, overlapping inner and outer edges of base by 1". Repeat until base is covered. Glue remaining items to wreath as desired, filling any gaps.

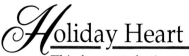

Holiday Heart

This fragrant, festive wreath recalls Christmas celebrations of bygone days.

MATERIALS

9"-long heart-shaped wire base
Brown florist's tape
100 dried rose hips (available at
  florist-supply stores)
Fifty cloves
250 tiny cedar cones
Forty-eight preserved holly leaves (available
  at florist-supply stores)
Two to three sprigs of pepper berries
Seventeen sprigs of preserved juniper
Hot glue gun and glue sticks
4½" length of jute

DIRECTIONS

1. Wrap base with florist's tape. Glue pairs
of rose hips to tape along middle of base,
butting top of one pair against bottom of next
pair. Glue remaining rose hips as desired atop
glued pairs to fill gaps. Reserving seven cedar
cones, glue remaining cones along inside
and outside edges of base, butting rose hips;
see photo.

2. Glue one or two cloves in center of each pair
of rose hips.

3. Glue forty-four holly leaves to back of base,
overlapping leaves slightly and arranging so
that tops of leaves extend beyond inside and
outside edges of base. Arrange remaining
holly leaves, pepper berries and juniper sprigs
in a spray. Glue to rose hips above cleavage of
heart; see photo. Glue reserved cedar cones to
center of spray.

4. To make hanger, knot ends of jute together.
Glue knot to back of wreath at bottom point of
heart cleavage.

Fruits of Christmas

Create a sparkling Della Robbia wreath suited for dining room or front door.

MATERIALS

22"-diameter wire base
Florist's wire
Fresh or artificial pine boughs
Hot glue gun and glue sticks
Plastic or wooden fruits: one grape bunch,
  two apples, two bananas, two oranges,
  two pears, two peaches, two lemons, four
  sets of two cherries, two plums
Nine plastic or wooden walnuts
Acrylic paints: yellow, red, light green, tan,
  brown, purple, peach, orange
Paintbrushes
Clear acrylic sealer spray
Shallow pan
Flaky glitter
White glue and glue brush

DIRECTIONS

1. Double one 14" length of florist's wire to make hanger. Make loop and wrap wire ends around base. Glue pine boughs to base, fanning boughs out at various angles.

2. Paint fruits and nuts as follows. Paint grapes and plums purple. Paint apples and cherries red. Paint bananas and lemons yellow, accenting bananas with light green and tan. Paint oranges orange. Paint pears light green, speckling with brown. Paint peaches peach, shading lightly with red. Paint walnuts tan, accenting with brown. Allow all to dry. Spray with clear sealer. Allow to dry.

3. Spread glitter in bottom of pan. Brush fruits and nuts one at a time with white glue. Roll in glitter to cover; allow to dry. Spray with clear sealer. Allow to dry.

4. Glue fruits and nuts to wreath; see diagram.

Diagram

Try This

Pinched for time? Purchase a fresh evergreen wreath at a nursery and ready-made papier mâché fruits at a craft store. Apply glitter to fruits as in Step 3. Glue fruits to the wreath.

Woodland Christmas Bounty

Colorful pepper berries complement the subtle, natural hues of a wreath that can be enjoyed in any season.

MATERIALS

16"-diameter grapevine base
4" length of dark green ¼"-wide
   polyester ribbon
Hot glue gun and glue sticks
Sprigs of preserved juniper
Two to three bunches of dried white statice
Three to four large bunches of pepper berries
Fifty to sixty dried cranberries*
Assorted dried seed pods: miniature bell cups,
   miniature lotus pods, poppy pods

*See "General Instructions" on page 126 for drying your own fruit.

DIRECTIONS

1. Make loop with polyester ribbon. Tie to base for hanger.

2. Glue four clusters of juniper sprigs, statice, pepper berries and cranberries to base. Layer items in this order: juniper sprigs, statice, pepper berries, cranberries. Glue remaining pepper berries along areas of base between the clusters.

3. Experiment with groupings of seed pods in each cluster; see photo for ideas. Glue pods to base.

Tiny Golden Treasure

In minutes, transform a collection of glittery buttons into a pretty miniature wreath just right for decorating the Christmas tree.

MATERIALS

1¼ yards of 14-gauge brass wire
About fifty ½"–1"-diameter, plain and
  embossed gold shank buttons
1¾ yards of 24-gauge brass wire
1½ yards of ⅛"-wide black/green/
  red-striped ribbon

Diagram

DIRECTIONS

1. Bend 14-gauge wire around itself to form a 3½"-diameter base; see diagram. Twist wire ends over completed base to secure.

2. Begin stringing buttons on 24-gauge wire. String loosely so that wire bends easily. Twist one end of wire tightly around base. Wrap base snugly with buttons on wire. Turn buttons so that some face inward and some outward, to give effect of fullness. Twist opposite end of wire tightly around base.

3. From ribbon, cut one 9" length and three 7" lengths. Reserve remaining ribbon. To make hanger, tie ends of 9" length around wire base, hiding knot under buttons. Tie 7" lengths in bows where desired on base. Tie one end of remaining ribbon to base near hanger. Cascade ribbon around wreath; see photo. Secure opposite end of ribbon to base, under buttons.

Bluebirds Galore

Charming little bluebirds add a woodlands appeal to this easy-to-make wreath.

MATERIALS

18"-diameter grapevine base
Artificial pine boughs
Hot glue gun and glue sticks
Twelve assorted large shelf and sponge
　mushrooms (available at
　florist-supply stores)
Eight twisted, varnished cane sticks
　(available at florist-supply stores)
Twelve dried peony pods
Four 5"–10"-long pieces of tree bark
Seven bluebirds

> ## ── Try This ──
>
> For a different look, replace the pine boughs, mushrooms, cane sticks and bark with dried or silk flowers entwined with silk ivy or geranium leaves. Perch the bluebirds along the vines.
>
> For a wedding-perfect wreath, add white doves instead of bluebirds. Use white and ivory flowers with white silk ribbon in place of the ivy.

DIRECTIONS

1. Glue pine boughs to base, fanning boughs over inside and outside edges.

2. Glue mushrooms, cane sticks and peony pods to wreath as desired; see photo for ideas. Glue bark to wreath, gluing largest piece at bottom center, like a shelf; see photo.

3. Glue birds to bark shelf, on mushrooms and among pine boughs of basic wreath as desired; see photo for ideas.

Miniature Beaded Beauty

Hang this sparkling miniature wreath in a window to reflect the radiant light of the season.

MATERIALS

3½ yards of 24-gauge brass wire
About 300 assorted beads: red, green and gold
   seed beads*; red and green bugle beads;
   round gold beads; red and green faceted
   beads; gold, red, clear and green
   pebble beads
Pencil or toothpick

*See "Suppliers" on page 128.

DIRECTIONS

  Begin stringing beads on wire about 1" from
one end; see photo for ideas. String beads
loosely so that wire bends easily. To make
wire curls, bend wire around pencil or toothpick, then continue adding beads until two-
thirds of wire is full. Form wire into a circle,
twisting beaded strand around itself; see
photo. Twist small loop in wire about 1" from
end for hanger, then twist wire ends together
to secure wreath shape.

Try This

  To make a miniature garland, string
the beads on the wire as described above,
but do not form into a circle. Cascade the
garland around a miniature Christmas
tree centerpiece.

 imple Celebration

Make a pretty Christmas star with simple materials and bright ribbon.

MATERIALS

1½"-thick x 12"-tall Styrofoam star
4" length of red polyester ribbon
Sheet moss
Hot glue gun and glue sticks
Thirty-six tiny cedar cones
Eight assorted pinecones
Ten sprigs of dried berries*
Eleven dried cranberries*
2¼ yards of ⅞"-wide red variegated
   wired ribbon
4" length of white florist's wire

*See "General Instructions" on page 126 for drying your own berries and cranberries.

DIRECTIONS

1. To make hanger, loop polyester ribbon and glue ends to back of star. Glue sheet moss to front, back and edges of star, covering Styrofoam and ribbon ends completely.

2. Experiment with clusters of pinecones, cedar cones, berry sprigs and cranberries on star front; see photo for ideas. Glue clusters in place.

3. From red variegated ribbon, cut one 58" length and ten 2" lengths. For bow, make twelve 2"-long loops in center of 58" ribbon length, leaving 5"-long tail on each side; see Diagram 1. Twist florist's wire tightly around loops about ½" from bottom; see Diagram 2. Fluff bow. Glue bow to star near top of one bottom point. Glue bow tails to star along bottom points, twisting as desired for ruffled effect. Notch ribbon ends.

4. Fold one 2" ribbon piece in half lengthwise. Glue to star among pinecones and cedar cones; see photo for placement. Repeat with remaining 2" ribbon lengths.

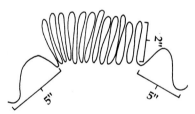

Diagram 1

Diagram 2

The Little Christmas Tree

Standing proudly in a grapevine arbor, this little tree shows off its treasures to the delight of all.

MATERIALS

16"-diameter grapevine base
10"-tall silk evergreen tree
Hot glue gun and glue sticks
One 1½"-tall wooden star cutout
Acrylic paint: yellow
Paintbrush
Eighteen ½" red plastic apples with hangers
Twelve 1"-tall straw baskets
1¾ yards of ⅛"-wide green/red/
   black-striped ribbon
6 yards of 2¼"-wide sheer, variegated
   red-striped ribbon
White florist's wire
4" length of ¼"-wide dark green
   polyester ribbon

DIRECTIONS

1. Prop base upright. Glue base of silk tree on inside edge of wreath at bottom center. Make sure tree stands straight; hold in place until glue sets.

2. Paint star cutout yellow. Allow to dry; set aside.

3. Cut ⅛"-wide ribbon into fifteen 4" lengths. Make a bow with each length. Snip ends of bow tails diagonally. Glue bows to ends of tree branches as desired. Hang baskets and apples on remaining tree branches; glue in place if desired. Glue star to top of tree.

4. For large bow, make twelve 5"–6"-long loops in 2¼"-wide ribbon, beginning about 14" from one end; see diagram. Wrap with florist's wire 1" from bottom of loops; secure. Fluff bow. Notch bow tails. Glue bow to wreath base below and to left of tree. Cascade bow tails along base, securing as needed with florist's wire or glue.

5. To make hanger, loop polyester ribbon and tie to back of base at top center.

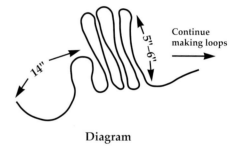

Diagram

Try This

Decorate the little tree with miniature toys, charms or hard candies. The little tree is also a perfect roost for tiny craft birds. Add a miniature craft bird's nest and a few sprigs of pepper berries to create a charming scene.

Once decorated, spray tree and base with silver or metallic gold paint for a glimmering holiday look.

Christmas Classic Stenciled Wreath

These painted evergreens and red berries will last for many holidays to come.

MATERIALS

Pencil
Mylar
Craft knife
7" x 11" piece of mat board
Drafting tape
Rubber cement
Acrylic paints: red, green
Metallic gold paint
Stencil brush

DIRECTIONS

1. The finished wreath will measure about 15½" x 15½". To make a smaller or larger wreath, reduce or enlarge patterns on copy machine. Surface to be stenciled should be clean and dry.

2. Transfer berry, greenery and Noel patterns on pages 46 and 47 to Mylar, allowing at least 3" between each. Cut out patterns, leaving space between each intact.

3. Tape berry and Noel patterns one at a time to mat board. Using craft knife, cut out areas to be stenciled. Reserve shape from area 1 of Noel. Tape greenery pattern to mat board; cut out and reserve areas 1, 2, 3, 4 and 5.

4. Position Noel stencil on desired surface where bottom center of wreath will be. Dab rubber cement on back of area 1 shape and press in position inside O. Do not let rubber cement extend beyond edge of shape. Carefully paint around shape with red, then stencil remainder of Noel with red. Allow to dry before lifting shape. To remove excess rubber cement, rub gently with small ball of dried rubber cement.

5. Position greenery stencil to left of Noel with edge B ⅞" from the N. Dab rubber cement on backs of areas 1, 2, 3, 4 and 5 and press in position inside greenery. Do not let rubber cement extend beyond edge of shapes. Carefully paint around shapes with green, then stencil remainder of greenery with green. Allow to dry before lifting shapes. Remove excess rubber cement as in Step 4. Repeat with greenery stencil and shapes to complete wreath; see Greenery Placement Diagram on page 47. Allow to dry.

6. Stencil red berries on greenery as desired; see photo for ideas. Allow to dry.

7. Accent each berry with metallic gold paint. Accent Noel letters with metallic gold and green.

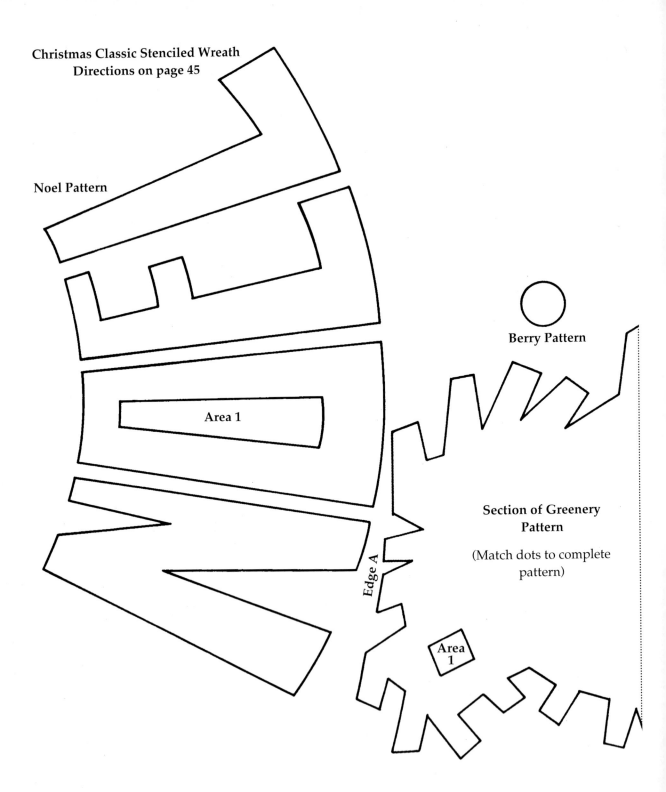

Christmas Classic Stenciled Wreath
Directions on page 45

Noel Pattern

Area 1

Berry Pattern

Section of Greenery
Pattern

(Match dots to complete
pattern)

Edge A

Area
1

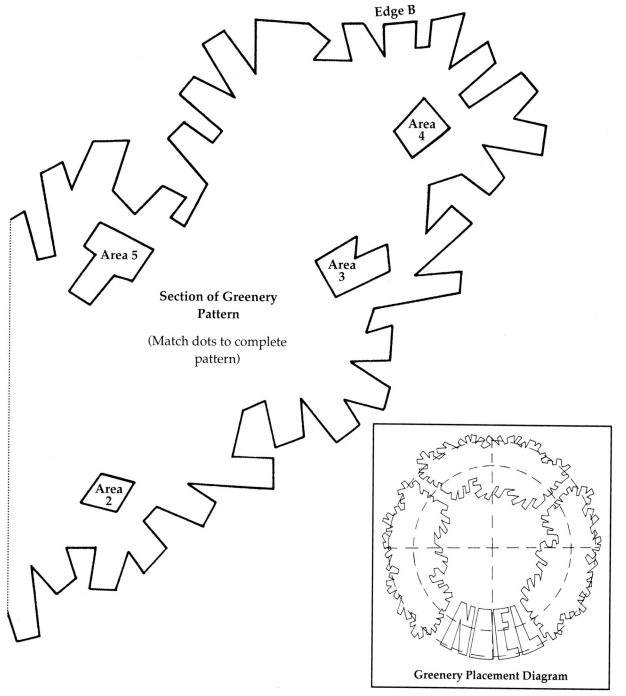

Edge B

Area
4

Area 5

Area
3

**Section of Greenery
Pattern**

(Match dots to complete
pattern)

Area
2

Greenery Placement Diagram

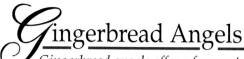

Gingerbread Angels

Gingerbread angels offer a fragrant and festive welcome to any room.

MATERIALS (for six angels)

Tracing paper
Lightweight paper
5 cups of all-purpose flour
1½ teaspoons of baking soda
2 teaspoons of ground ginger
1 teaspoon of ground cloves
½ teaspoon of salt
1 cup of shortening
1 cup of sugar
One egg
1 cup of molasses
2 tablespoons of vinegar
Wax paper
Rolling pin with cloth cover
Craft knife or plastic orange peeler
Large mixing bowl
Cookie sheet
Wire rack
One tube of white embroidery paint

DIRECTIONS

1. Trace angel pattern. Transfer to paper. Cut out and set aside.

2. Stir together flour, baking soda, spices and salt. In large mixing bowl, beat shortening for 30 seconds by hand or with mixer. Add sugar; beat until light. Add egg, molasses and vinegar; beat well. Add dry ingredients. Blend thoroughly, then beat well. Cover and refrigerate for 3 hours or overnight.

3. Preheat oven to 375°F. Grease cookie sheet. Place wax paper on work surface under dough. Using rolling pin, roll dough to ⅛" thickness. Dip paper pattern into flour; shake off excess. Place pattern on rolled dough. Using craft knife or plastic orange peeler, cut out six angels. Smooth edges with fingers as needed.

4. Place angels 1" apart on cookie sheet. Bake 5–6 minutes. Cool for 1 minute, then remove to wire rack.

5. Using embroidery paint according to manufacturer's instructions, add details to angels; see pattern. These angels are non-edible. For edible angels, paint details with pastry icing and do not glue angels to wreath.

MATERIALS (for wreath)

Six decorated gingerbread angels
17"-diameter flat grapevine base
Hot glue gun and glue sticks
6" length of jute

DIRECTIONS

1. Place base on flat surface. Glue angels to base with wing tips about ⅛" apart and heads inward.

2. To make hanger, loop jute and tie ends to back of base where desired.

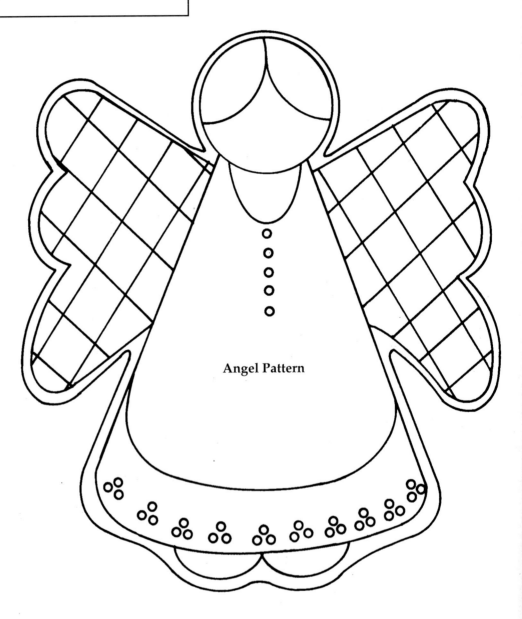

Angel Pattern

Opposite: Noah's Gingerbread Ark

*N*oah's Gingerbread Ark

Noah and his animal shipmates parade around their ark on this delightful wreath. (Project pictured on previous page.)

MATERIALS (for animals, Noah and ark)

Tracing paper
Lightweight paper
5 cups of all-purpose flour
1½ teaspoons of baking soda
2 teaspoons of ground ginger
1 teaspoon of ground cloves
½ teaspoon of salt
1 cup of shortening
1 cup of sugar
One egg
1 cup of molasses
2 tablespoons of vinegar
Wax paper
Rolling pin with cloth cover
Craft knife or plastic orange peeler
Large mixing bowl
Toothpick
Metal teaspoon
Cookie sheet
Wire rack

DIRECTIONS

1. Trace animal, Noah and ark patterns on pages 53, 54 and 55. Transfer to paper. Cut out and set aside.

2. Stir together flour, baking soda, spices and salt. In large mixing bowl, beat shortening for 30 seconds by hand or with mixer. Add sugar; beat until light. Add egg, molasses and vinegar; beat well. Add dry ingredients. Blend thoroughly, then beat well. Cover and refrigerate for 3 hours or overnight.

3. Preheat oven to 375°F. Grease cookie sheet. Divide dough and keep unused portions refrigerated to prevent drying. Place wax paper on work surface under dough. Using rolling pin, roll dough to ⅛" thickness. Dip paper patterns into flour; shake off excess. Place patterns on rolled dough. Using craft knife or plastic orange peeler, cut out one ark, one Noah and two of each animal. Smooth edges with fingers as needed. Using toothpick and teaspoon, add details to ark according to pattern.

4. Place shapes 1" apart on cookie sheet. Bake 5–6 minutes. Cool for 1 minute, then remove to wire rack.

MATERIALS (for wreath)

Gingerbread animals, Noah and ark
16"-diameter wire base
Artificial pine boughs with wire stems
Seven large, red cockscombs (available at florist-supply stores)
Twenty-two 5"–6"-long cinnamon sticks
Hot glue gun and glue sticks
3⅞ yards of 1½"-wide burgundy wired ribbon with metallic gold edges
Green florist's wire

DIRECTIONS

1. To make hanger, cut one 14" length of florist's wire. Double to make one 7" length. Loop doubled wire and wrap tails around wire base at back where top of wreath will be.

2. Cover wire base by wrapping stems of pine boughs around it. Fluff boughs and trim as needed for full effect.

3. Nestle cockscombs among pine boughs about 7" apart; glue in place. Group cinnamon sticks in threes and fours and glue beside cockscombs; see photo for placement.

4. Glue ark to bottom center of wreath. Glue Noah to right of ark. Glue animals, two by two, around wreath as desired; see photo for ideas.

5. From ribbon, cut one 2⅞-yard length for bow. Make ten 4½"-long loops in center of ribbon length, leaving about 6"-long tails. Wrap bow tightly with a 10" length of florist's wire ½" above bottoms of loops; do not cut wire tails. Fluff bow and notch bow tails. Make streamer with remaining ribbon, twisting as desired and gluing to pine boughs; see photo for ideas. Notch streamer ends. Using tails of florist's wire, wire bow to wreath at center of streamer. Twist bow tails as desired; glue to pine boughs.

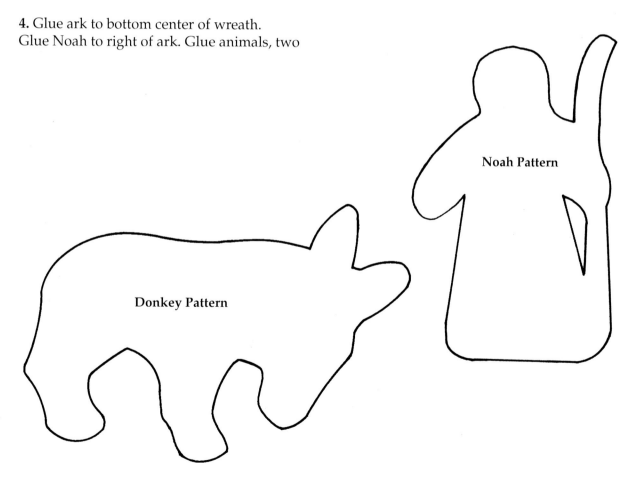

Noah Pattern

Donkey Pattern

53

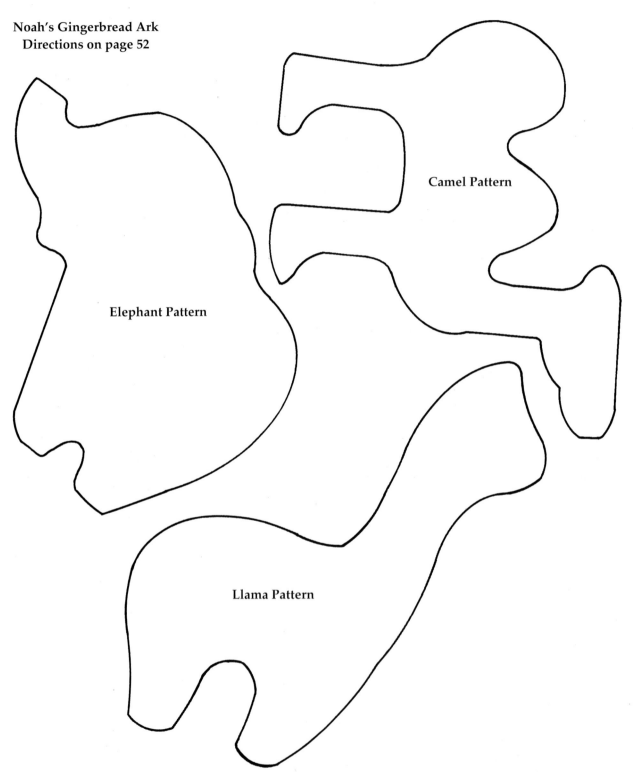

Noah's Gingerbread Ark
Directions on page 52

Camel Pattern

Elephant Pattern

Llama Pattern

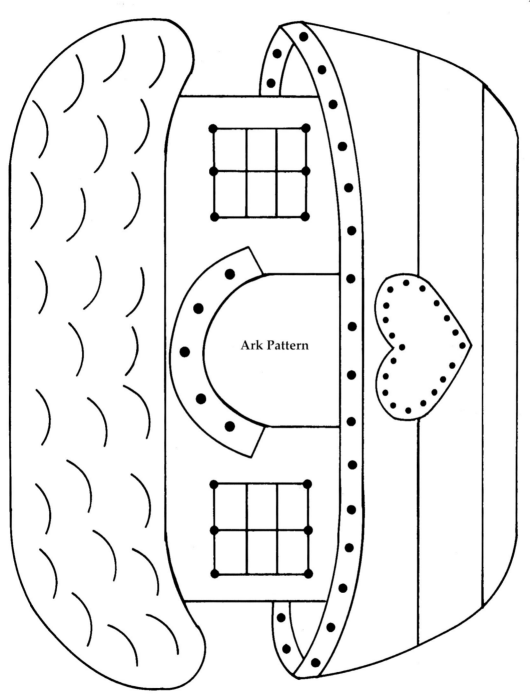

Ark Pattern

$\mathcal{H}$ave a Chocolate Christmas!

Top a holiday cake with this edible wreath, or present it in a candy box as a delectable gift.

MATERIALS

Cookie sheet
Wax paper
Ten 1¼"-long plain chocolate eggs
Small knife
One 16-ounce brick of dipping chocolate
Double boiler
Nonstick spray coating
Candy mold with 1½"-long leaf shapes

Diagram

DIRECTIONS

1. Cover cookie sheet with wax paper. Using knife and beginning at large end of one chocolate egg, cut shallow scallops around egg to resemble pinecone seed covers; see diagram. Turn each scallop back slightly. Repeat with remaining chocolate eggs. Place eggs on cookie sheet in cool, dry location.

2. Spray candy mold with nonstick spray coating. Set aside a small portion of dipping chocolate for "glue." In double boiler over low to medium heat, melt remaining dipping chocolate until smooth. Do not overheat chocolate. Spoon melted chocolate into candy mold. Make twenty-six leaves. Cool leaves completely before removing from mold. Place on cookie sheet.

3. To assemble wreath, arrange leaves in a 4¼"-diameter circle on wax paper, with all leaves pointing clockwise and some overlapping. Melt portion of reserved chocolate to glue leaves together; melt remaining chocolate to glue chocolate pinecones to wreath as desired; see photo for ideas.

$\mathcal{T}$ry This

Add silver or multicolor nonpareils to the wreath by pressing them gently into the chocolate. Make a peppermint and chocolate wreath with white chocolate; crush peppermint candies into the chocolate as it melts for a colorful, holiday-perfect look.

Apple Village Christmas

Create a wreath as inviting as a snowy, hometown holiday.

MATERIALS

16"-diameter grapevine, Styrofoam
  or wire base
Artificial pine boughs with wire stems
Hot glue gun and glue sticks
One 2" x 2¾" wooden house with chimney*
Two 1½" x 3" wooden houses with chimneys*
Two 1¼"-tall wooden tree cutouts
Three ¾" wooden star cutouts
Three 1¼" wooden star cutouts
Four ½" wooden heart cutouts
Three 1⅝" wooden heart cutouts
Acrylic paints: cream, light green, light blue,
  brown, dark brown, dark red, green, olive
  green, dark gray, tan, black, white
Paintbrushes
Thirty ½"-long red plastic apples with
  silk leaves
Nine sprigs of silk holly
5 yards of 4½"-wide red paper ribbon
Thread

*Available at craft and hobby stores

DIRECTIONS

1. Cut pine boughs into 3"–4" lengths. Glue to base in a clockwise direction, with tops overlapping ends. Fill in along inside and outside edges of base.

2. Paint details on fronts and sides of houses; see Diagram 1 and Color Key on page 60. Allow to dry. Paint one tree light green and one light blue. Paint each small star light blue, brown, red or light green. Paint each large star brown or cream. Paint each small heart light blue, red or light green. Paint each large heart cream or red. Allow all to dry.

3. Glue houses together side by side; see photo. Glue one small heart to one lobe of one large heart and one to top of one tree. Glue another small heart to lower right point of one large star. Glue one small star to left edge of large heart with small star. Glue another small star to left edge of another large heart. Reserve remaining hearts and stars.

4. Glue bottom of houses to bottom center of wreath. Experiment with grouping remaining items on the wreath, using wooden cutouts, apples and holly sprigs; see photo for ideas. Glue groupings in place.

5. For small bows, cut six 6" lengths from paper ribbon. Make three equal loops in one length. Wrap tightly with thread ½" from bottom of loops; secure. Fluff bow. Glue to wreath where desired. Repeat with remaining 6" ribbon lengths.

6. For large bow, make eleven equal loops in remaining length of paper ribbon, beginning 5" from one end; see Diagram 2. Wrap tightly with thread ½" from bottom of loops; secure. Fluff bow. Notch ribbon tails. Glue bow to wreath, cascading ribbon tails; see photo for placement.

Apple Village Christmas
Directions on page 59

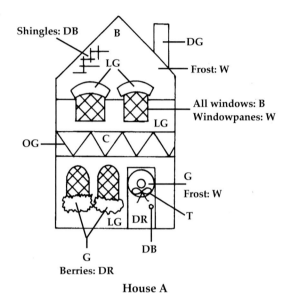

Shingles: DB
B
DG
LG
Frost: W
All windows: B
Windowpanes: W
LG
OG
C
G
Frost: W
T
LG
DR
DB
G
Berries: DR

House A

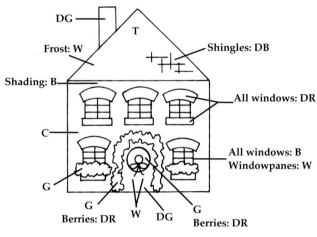

DG
T
Frost: W
Shingles: DB
Shading: B
All windows: DR
C
All windows: B
Windowpanes: W
G
G
G
Berries: DR
W
DG
Berries: DR

House B

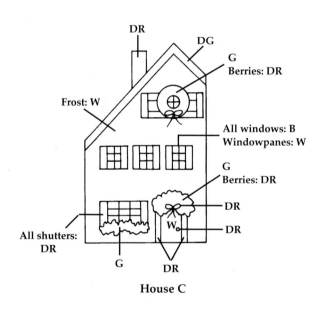

DR
DG
G
Berries: DR
Frost: W
All windows: B
Windowpanes: W
G
Berries: DR
DR
DR
All shutters: DR
W
G
DR

House C

Color Key			
B	= Brown	G	= Green
DB	= Dark brown	LG	= Light green
T	= Tan	OG	= Olive green
C	= Cream	LB	= Light blue
DG	= Dark gray	W	= White
DR	= Dark red	BL	= Black

Diagram 1

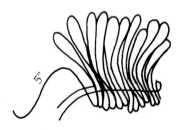

5"

Diagram 2

Opposite: Roses and Ivy

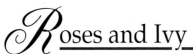

Roses and Ivy

This elegant, everlasting topiary is simple to create. (Project pictured on previous page.)

MATERIALS

8½"-diameter topiary frame with 4"-long
  supports (available at garden stores)
6"-diameter x 4½"-tall flowerpot
One 4½" x 26" piece of 2"-thick batting
Spray adhesive
1 yard of white velveteen
Hot glue gun and glue sticks
One 6" x 6" piece of 2"-thick Styrofoam
Paring knife
5' of silk ivy with bendable stem
Green florist's wire
Wire cutters
Sheet moss
Needle and white thread
Metallic gold silk rose leaves with stems
Tracing paper
Scrap of cardboard
White polymer clay
Wax paper
Rolling pin
Paring knife
Round toothpick
Metallic gold paint
Sponge
Nylon filament thread

DIRECTIONS

1. Lightly coat sides of flowerpot with spray adhesive. Wrap pot in batting. Trim excess batting from rim of pot and trim flush with bottom edge of pot. From velveteen, cut one 25" x 25" piece; set aside remaining fabric. Center pot on wrong side of fabric. Draw fabric firmly up over pot so that it is smooth and tight across pot bottom. Gather fabric loosely over batting and along pot rim. Tuck ends inside pot, gluing in place.

2. Using paring knife, trim Styrofoam to fit snugly inside bottom of pot. Place in pot.

3. Beginning at one support of topiary frame and ending at opposite support, twine ivy around frame; see Diagram 1. Repeat back and forth around frame until frame is completely covered. Use short lengths of florist's wire as needed to secure ivy to frame. Arrange ivy leaves to hide wire. Insert topiary frame supports into Styrofoam piece until bottom curve of topiary frame is level with rim of pot; see Diagram 2. Fill pot with sheet moss.

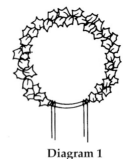

Diagram 1

Diagram 2

4. For roses, cut remaining velveteen into 1½"-diameter circles. To make a rosebud, roll one circle into a spiral and secure by sewing across bottom end; see Diagram 3. To make a rose, follow directions for a rosebud, then add petals by sewing a tuck in bottom half of one circle and bending top half back; see Diagram 4. Fold petal around rose center; see Diagram 4. Glue. Continue adding petals in layers until rose is about 2" in diameter. Repeat to make second rose. Glue rosebud to petal of one completed rose. Glue roses in a cluster to front of velveteen-covered flowerpot. Arrange silk rose leaves as desired and glue behind rose cluster.

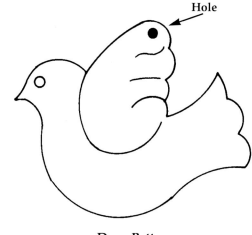

Dove Pattern

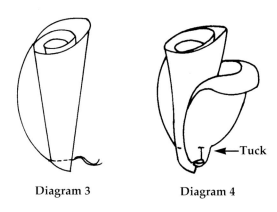

Diagram 3   Diagram 4

6. Sponge-paint both sides of two doves lightly with metallic gold paint. From florist's wire, cut one 4½" length. Glue wire to center back of dove without hole in wing, ½" from bottom edge. Insert opposite end of wire through sheet moss and into Styrofoam in pot. From nylon thread, cut two 3" lengths. Loop thread through wing holes of two remaining doves and tie ornaments to topiary frame where desired.

5. Trace dove pattern opposite, transferring all information. Transfer pattern to cardboard. Cut out. Work clay with hands until warm and pliable. Place between two sheets of wax paper. Using rolling pin, roll clay until about ¼" thick. Remove top sheet of wax paper. Place dove pattern on clay. Using paring knife, cut out three doves. Using toothpick, add eyes and wing details according to pattern. Also use toothpick to make hole through wing of two doves according to pattern. Bake clay according to manufacturer's instructions. Allow to cool.

Try This

Cover the flowerpot with fabric that matches your drapes or upholstery; make the roses from complementary fabric. Tassels may be glued to the pot cover under the rose cluster; see "General Instructions" on page 126 for making tassels.

Wire small silk flowers and leaves to the topiary frame in addition to, or in place of, the ivy.

Season's "Wheat"ings!

Combine the traditional look of wheat art and salt dough sculpture for a delightful choir of angels crowned with harvest gold.

MATERIALS (for one angel)

Tracing paper
Lightweight paper
½ cup of hot water
¼ cup of salt
Mixing bowl
1 cup of all-purpose flour
Rolling pin
Paring knife
Bamboo skewer
Plastic wrap
Aluminum foil
Cookie sheet
Wire rack
Acrylic paints: yellow, red, green, light blue,
  dark blue, pink
Fruitwood water-base wood stain
Paintbrushes

DIRECTIONS

1. Trace angel patterns on page 67, transferring all information. Transfer to lightweight paper; cut out. Set aside.

2. Pour hot water and salt into bowl. Stir for 1 minute. The salt grains will reduce but not dissolve. Add flour and stir until water is absorbed. Knead dough for 5–10 minutes or longer, adding a little flour if dough is sticky.

3. Roll dough out to ¼" thickness. Place angel patterns on dough. Using paring knife, cut out one back, one set of wings, one dress with arms and one hymnal. Make two 6"-long thin tubes of dough. Attach along outside edges of each angel wing to form wing rim; see pattern. Add details to wings and dress, using flat end of skewer to make indentations. Score hymnal according to pattern. Cover all with plastic wrap and set aside.

4. For angel head, make ball of dough about 1⅛" in diameter and ¾" thick. Flatten slightly. Make hair from four small tubes of dough curved and flattened against head and make bangs from three small tubes of dough; see Face Guide on page 67. Add eyelashes with pointed end of skewer. Make mouth with fingertip or handle of paring knife. Place angel head under plastic wrap.

5. For halo, make 3"-long tube of dough. Gently twist tube; see Halo Guide on page 67. Preheat oven to 200°F.

6. Cover work surface with sheet of foil. To assemble angel, moisten backs of all pieces with hot water, then gently press together as follows. Attach wings to back, matching outside edges. Curve halo and attach to back below cutout areas; see photo. Attach dress with arms to back, matching scalloped edges. Attach head at top of dress and center of wings. Curve arms to center and secure with a little water. Attach hymnal to arms where they meet.

7. Lift foil with assembled angel onto cookie sheet. Bake for 4 hours or until dough is completely dry and hard. Remove to wire rack and allow to cool completely.

8. Paint angel hair yellow. Paint hymnal light blue. Paint cheeks and mouth pink. Paint eyelashes dark blue. Paint indentations in wings and dress red and green. Allow to dry. Brush angel with wood stain, then immediately use clean brush to dab off excess stain, allowing paint colors to show through. Allow to dry.

9. Repeat Steps 2–8 to make additional angels.

MATERIALS (for wreath)

Five painted salt dough angels
18"-diameter open-weave rattan base with 5"-
    diameter solid-weave center and 1½"-wide
    solid-weave band near edge
One large bundle of dried, ripe wheat
    with 12"–14"-long stems
Monofilament thread
Hot glue gun and glue sticks
Scissors
6 yards of 6"-wide red paper ribbon

DIRECTIONS

1. Separate wheat into five bundles of eighteen to twenty stalks each. Using monofilament, bind each bundle together 4¼" below wheat heads. Place rattan base on flat surface. With binding over solid-weave band, place one bundle at 12 o'clock position on base, one at 2 o'clock position, one at 5 o'clock position, one at 7 o'clock and one at 10 o'clock, overlapping ends of stalks; see Diagram 1. Fan stalks out from binding to create star shape; see photo. Trim stalks to about 12" in length so ends are within solid-weave center of base. Glue each

bundle in place on solid-weave band, binding to rattan with monofilament if needed to secure.

2. Center and glue one angel on each bundle; see photo for placement.

3. Open out paper ribbon and cut in half lengthwise, making two 3"-wide strips 6 yards long. Cut five 1-yard lengths; reserve remaining ribbon. Tie each 1-yard length into a bow. Fluff bow and notch ribbon tails. Glue bows to solid-weave band between angels with bow tails inward.

4. Compress remaining ribbon to ¾" width. Glue one end to back of solid-weave center between 10 o'clock and 12 o'clock wheat stalks. Keeping even tension, weave ribbon back and forth across wreath center, over stalks and under rattan, forming star shape; see Diagram 2. Glue end of ribbon to back of solid-weave center.

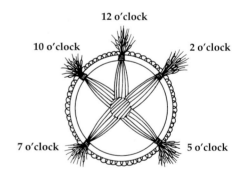

Diagram 1

Diagram 2

5. To make hanger, cut one 12" length of monofilament thread. Double to make one 6" length. Insert ends through rattan scallop behind one angel. Knot ends around rattan.

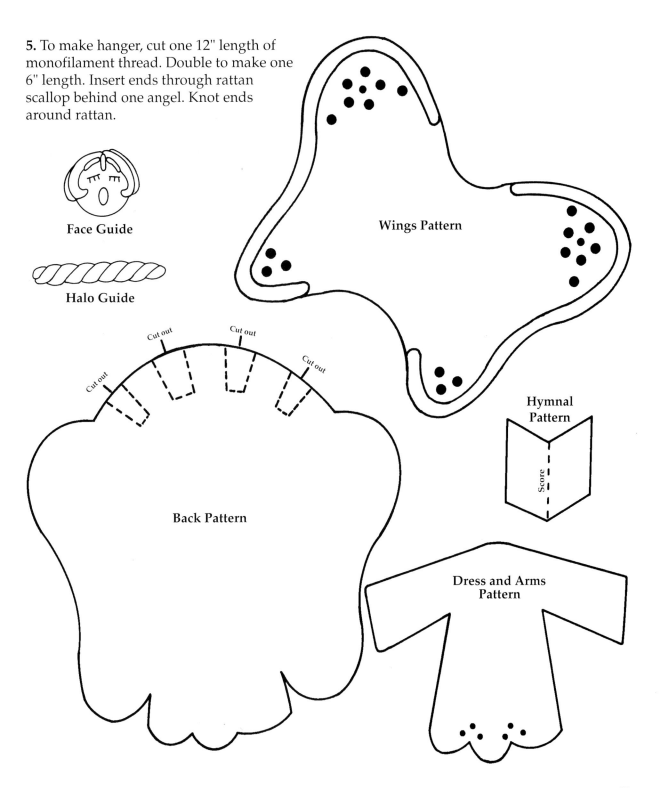

Face Guide

Halo Guide

Wings Pattern

Hymnal Pattern

Score

Cut out

Cut out

Cut out

Cut out

Back Pattern

Dress and Arms Pattern

Festive Floral Fantasy

Transform pretty paper napkins into fantastic Christmas flowers, leaves and bright berries in just a few minutes.

MATERIALS

12"-diameter straw base
4 yards of 3½"-wide green paper ribbon
Hot glue gun and glue sticks
Eighteen 12⅞" x 12⅞" red/green floral
   print paper napkins
Eighteen 3"-long, pale yellow artificial
   stamen groupings
Toothpick
Craft wire
Fifteen 9¾" x 9¾" green floral print
   paper napkins
Six 9¾" x 9¾" red floral print paper napkins
Twenty-four ¾"-diameter foam balls
Thread

DIRECTIONS

1. Open out paper ribbon. Glue one end to straw base; allow glue to dry. Wrap base with ribbon, overlapping wraps by ½" and ending where wrapping began. Glue opposite end of ribbon in place.

2. Open out one red/green print napkin. To make a flower, use toothpick to poke hole in center of napkin. Insert one stamen grouping in hole. Secure in place with edges of hole gathered around it by wrapping with thread; see Diagram 1A. Secure thread. Gently bring all four corners of napkin to back and gather over wrapped portion of stamen grouping; see Diagram 1B. Wrap with wire and secure; see Diagram 1C. Fluff flower. Trim excess paper

below wrapping. Repeat with remaining red/green print napkins and stamen groupings.

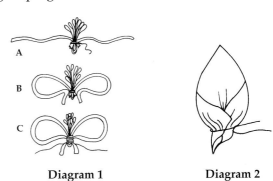

Diagram 1   Diagram 2

3. To make a leaf, cut one green print napkin in four pieces along folds. Roll two corners of one piece toward center of piece. Gather and twist lower end of piece slightly; see Diagram 2. Wrap lower end with thread and secure. Trim excess paper below wrapping. Repeat with remaining green print napkins.

4. To make a berry, cut one red print napkin in four pieces along folds. Place one foam ball in center of one piece. Wrap paper around foam ball, gathering edges so paper fits snugly around ball. Wrap with thread and secure. Trim excess paper below wrapping. Repeat with remaining red print napkins and foam balls.

5. Glue flowers to base first. Glue leaves to base as desired, filling in around flowers. Glue berries to leaves, flowers or base in clusters of two or three; see photo for ideas.

Heartfelt Christmas Wish

Delight family and friends with the old-fashioned flair of this easy-to-make garland.

MATERIALS (for hearts)

Tracing paper
Lightweight paper
Mylar
5 cups of all-purpose flour
1½ teaspoons of baking soda
2 teaspoons of ground ginger
1 teaspoon of ground cloves
½ teaspoon of salt
1 cup of shortening
1 cup of sugar
One egg
1 cup of molasses
2 tablespoons of vinegar
Wax paper
Rolling pin with cloth cover
Craft knife
Large mixing bowl
Cookie sheet
Wire rack
Acrylic paints: red, green, white
Paintbrushes

DIRECTIONS

1. Trace heart and holly patterns on page 72. Transfer to paper. Cut out and set aside. Transfer to Mylar. Using craft knife, cut out areas to be stenciled; set aside.

2. Stir together flour, baking soda, spices and salt. In large mixing bowl, beat shortening for 30 seconds by hand or with mixer. Add sugar; beat until light. Add egg, molasses and vinegar; beat well. Add dry ingredients. Blend thoroughly, then beat well. Cover and refrigerate for three hours or overnight.

3. Preheat oven to 375°F. Grease cookie sheet. Place wax paper on work surface under dough. Using rolling pin, roll dough to ⅛" thickness. Dip paper heart pattern into flour; shake off excess. Place pattern on rolled dough. Using craft knife, cut out fourteen hearts. Smooth edges with fingers as needed.

4. Place hearts 1" apart on cookie sheet. Bake 5–6 minutes. Cool for 1 minute, then remove to wire rack. Cool completely.

5. Stencil holly on left lobe of each heart near edge, painting leaves green and berries red. Using white paint and Actual-Size Letter Guide on page 73, paint one letter on each heart to spell out Merry Christmas. Note: Painted hearts are nonedible and should be kept out of reach of small children and pets.

MATERIALS (for garland)

Fourteen decorated gingerbread hearts
6'-long artificial pine bough swag
15'-long string of popcorn
Twenty-four red plastic berry sticks with
  ½"-diameter berries
Hot glue gun and glue sticks

DIRECTIONS

1. Extend swag to full length and place on flat surface. Beginning about 5" from one end, loop string of popcorn around garland, securing with glue as needed and finishing about 5" from opposite end of swag.

2. Glue decorated gingerbread hearts to garland between or over popcorn loops, spelling out Merry Christmas; see diagram.

3. Glue berry sticks to garland as desired, hiding ends among greenery; see photo for ideas.

Try This

Spell out holiday greetings in different languages, such as Glad Jul, Feliz Navidad or Joyeux Noel. Or spell out family names on the hearts. Use a purchased stencil alphabet, available in many styles of lettering from plain to ornate. Try painting the letters in metallic gold for a different look.

Decorate the hearts with glued-on beads, buttons, bows or silk holly or spray paint them gold or silver.

Diagram

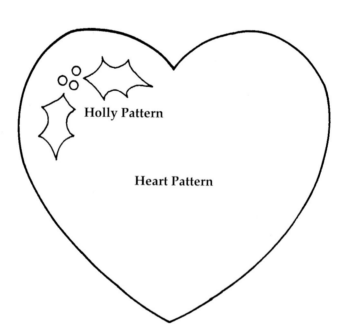

Holly Pattern

Heart Pattern

MERY

CHI

STA

Actual-Size Letter Guide

Heartfelt Christmas Wish
Directions on page 71

_I_talian Holiday Elegance

The subtle colors of this wreath in the classic Della Robbia style will blend beautifully with any holiday decor.

MATERIALS

4 cups of all-purpose flour
1 cup of salt
1½ cups of water
Spray bottle of water
Large mixing bowl
Plastic wrap
Aluminum foil
Rolling pin
Paring knife
Whole cloves
Toothpicks
Fork
Cookie sheet
Wire rack
Varnish or shellac
Paintbrush
Epoxy cement

DIRECTIONS

1. Blend flour and salt in mixing bowl. Add 1½ cups of water to flour mixture. Mix thoroughly with hands. Knead until smooth. Roll into ball and cover with plastic wrap.

2. Preheat oven to 300°F. Pinch off about 2 cups of dough. Roll into a ½"-thick sausage shape. Pat sausage down with hands to about 1½" wide. On large piece of aluminum foil, form sausage into an 8"-diameter circle with about a 5"-diameter center opening. Moisten

sausage ends with spray bottle and overlap slightly. Press together, smoothing surface with fingers. Cover with plastic wrap.

3. To decorate wreath, pinch off pieces of dough and flatten with hands to about ¼" thickness. Using paring knife, cut out leaf and petal shapes; see Wreath Decoration Guide on page 76. Use toothpick to add leaf veins. Overlap petals slightly and press together to make flowers. Make flower centers from twelve to fourteen tiny pellets of dough; press cluster of pellets into middle of each flower. Add details to petals with toothpick or fork. Moisten lightly with spray bottle; cover with plastic wrap until ready to attach to wreath.

4. Make one apple, three pears, ten small strawberries, two peaches and about sixty-six cherries next, using pinches of dough in desired sizes; see Wreath Decoration Guide on page 76. Press whole cloves into dough for stems of fruits. Add textures and details with toothpick or fork. Remove plastic wrap from wreath and moisten with spray bottle. Attach fruits, leaves and flowers, leaving space at bottom center of wreath for bow; see photo for placement ideas. Fill in with clusters of cherries; use toothpick to indent top of each cherry. Reserve a dozen cherries to decorate bow. Make vine tendrils from 1/16"-wide sausages of dough; curl and curve over fruits; see photo. Reserve ¾ cup of dough to make bow. Moisten wreath lightly with spray bottle; cover with plastic wrap.

5. To make bow, roll out reserved dough to ¼" thickness. Cut out a 20"–24"-long strip about 1¼" wide. Fold and pinch strip into bow with tails. Make bow knot with short strip of dough, folding ends to back of bow. Notch bow tails. Use toothpick to add folds on either side of knot. Moisten backs of reserved cherries and attach to bow knot and along one bow tail. Remove plastic wrap from wreath. Moisten back of decorated bow and attach to space at bottom center of wreath. Arrange bow shape as desired. If needed, fill in around bow with any remaining dough in cherry or leaf shapes.

6. Lift aluminum foil with wreath onto cookie sheet. Bake for 3 hours or until completely dry and hard. If any portions become done earlier, cover with scrap of aluminum foil to protect from burning.

7. Place wreath on wire rack and allow to cool. Place rack in dry area and leave wreath for several days. Peel aluminum foil from back of wreath. Lightly coat front with varnish or shellac. Allow to dry. Turn; coat back with varnish or shellac. If any portions break off, repair with epoxy cement. (Dough wreaths are nonedible once varnished or shellacked. Keep out of reach of small children and pets.)

Try This

To give the wreath a deep golden color, stir 1 teaspoon of instant tea into 1½ cups of warm water. Allow to cool before adding to flour mixture as in Step 1. Food coloring may be added to the dough in the same way.

Lightly spray the wreath with metallic gold paint for a rich, gilded effect. For still another look, after cooling, paint the fruits, vine tendrils and bow with food paints in realistic or fantasy hues, then shellac or varnish the wreath.

Individual fruits are charming as hanging ornaments. Use a toothpick to poke a hole through the top of the fruit before baking. Decorate the fruit ornaments with metallic spray or food paint, or leave them natural. Hang the ornaments with loops of gold cord.

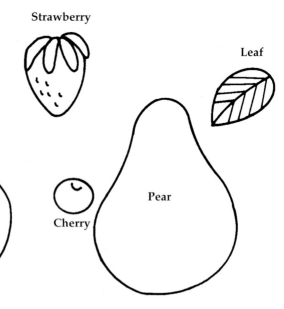

Strawberry

Leaf

Flower

Peach/Plum

Cherry

Pear

Wreath Decoration Guide

76

Opposite: Elves Galore

Elves Galore

Santa's happy elves peek from their perches on this pretty wreath. (Project pictured on previous page.)

MATERIALS (for basic wreath)

18"-diameter grapevine base
Artificial pine boughs
Hot glue gun and glue sticks
Twelve assorted large shelf and sponge
   mushrooms (available at
   florist-supply stores)
Eight twisted, varnished cane sticks
   (available at florist-supply stores)
Twelve dried peony pods
Four 5"–10"-long pieces of tree bark

DIRECTIONS

1. Glue pine boughs to base, fanning boughs over inside and outside edges.

2. Glue mushrooms, cane sticks and peony pods to wreath as desired; see photo for ideas. Glue bark to wreath, gluing largest piece at bottom center, like a shelf; see photo.

MATERIALS (for six elves)

Six 2½"-tall unpainted, wooden spool dolls
   without arms or legs
Acrylic paints: white, black, coral, raw sienna
Small paintbrushes
Two 4" x 14" pieces of green/red/white
   print fabric
Three 3" x 3½" pieces of red print fabric;
   matching thread
Hot glue gun and glue sticks
Two 4" lengths of ⅜"-wide green chenille stem

Three 4" lengths of ⅜"-wide white
   chenille stem
One 4" length of ⅜"-wide red chenille stem
Three ½"-diameter white pom-poms
One ½"-diameter green pom-pom
Two ½"-diameter red pom-poms
16" length of ¹⁄₁₆"-wide green ribbon
16" length of ¹⁄₁₆"-wide white ribbon
16" length of ¹⁄₁₆"-wide red/black/green-
   striped ribbon

DIRECTIONS

1. Paint spool doll body white. Following Elf Face Guide, paint one ⅛"-diameter white dot for each eye. Allow to dry. Add smaller black dot in each eye for pupils. Paint thin black line around top edge of each eye and paint eye-lashes, nose and mouth with black. Allow to dry. Using dry brush, dab cheeks with coral. Paint freckles with raw sienna. Add one white dot to each eye pupil for highlights. Allow to dry.

2. From green/red/white fabric, cut one 2" x 14" strip and one 2" x 5" strip. To make legs, fold long edges of 2" x 14" strip toward center ½"; see Diagrams 1A and 1B. Press. Fold strip in half lengthwise; see Diagram 1C. Press. Tie knot about ½" from each end of strip. Cut strip in half; set aside.

3. To make arms, repeat folding instructions in Step 2, using 2" x 5" fabric strip. Tie knot in center of strip.

78

Elf Face Guide

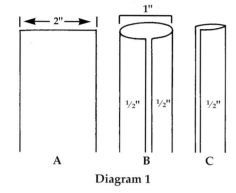

Diagram 1

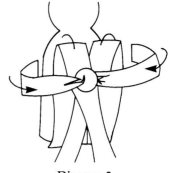

Diagram 2

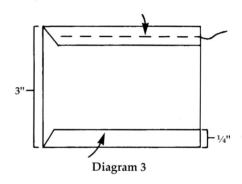

Diagram 3

4. Glue unknotted ends of legs, one over the other, to spool doll bottom. Bring legs up to spool doll front and fold over below head with "knees" together and legs crossed; see Diagram 2. Center knot in arms over legs about ¼" below spool doll neck; see Diagram 2. Pull arm ends to back of spool doll, turning under as needed for snug fit; glue.

5. To make hat, fold long edges of red print fabric in ¼" on each edge to make 3" x 3" square; see Diagram 3. Beginning at back of doll, glue one folded short edge of fabric to doll head, keeping front of hat above painted eyes. Sew gathering thread around opposite edge of hat; see Diagram 3. Tighten thread and secure. To make hat cuff, glue green chenille stem over edge of hat, beginning and ending at back of doll head. Glue white pom-pom at tip of hat. Fold hat over; glue end to doll head.

6. Cut one 8" length of green ribbon. Tie ribbon in a bow around doll neck.

7. To make the five additional elves shown on the basic wreath, repeat Steps 1–5. Paint one body white, two bodies red and two green. Use different colors of fabric for each set of arms and legs and for each hat. Use green chenille stem for one hat cuff, red for one and white for three. Use two white pom-poms, two red pom-poms and one green pom-pom. Use a different color of ribbon for each additional elf's bow. Using glue, "seat" elves on bark shelf, on mushrooms and among pine boughs of basic wreath.

tarry Winter Night

Create a country-style copper wreath to gleam in kitchen or breakfast nook.

MATERIALS

2 yards of 24-gauge copper wire
8 yards of 14-gauge copper wire
Pliers
Tracing paper
One 5" x 20" sheet of 36-gauge tooling copper
Ballpoint pen
Old scissors
⅛"-diameter tin punch
Soldering iron; soldering wire with resin core
Soft cotton cloth

DIRECTIONS

1. To make wreath base, draw an 8¾"-diameter circle on tracing paper. Form 24-gauge wire to fit around circle; wrap wire eight times around and bend ends to secure. Twist 14-gauge wire around 24-gauge wire circle, making sure to keep circle shape symmetrical. Using pliers, bend ends to secure.

2. Trace star and moon patterns opposite, transferring all information. Cut out. Using ballpoint pen, outline fifteen stars and one moon on tooling copper. Also use ballpoint pen to draw lines on stars and indicate location of holes. Using scissors, cut out stars and moon.

3. Using tin punch, punch holes in stars and moon.

4. Solder stars to wreath base in groups of two to four, leaving a space for moon and single star; see photo for ideas. Solder moon and single star to base.

5. Use cotton cloth to lightly erase any finger marks on copper.

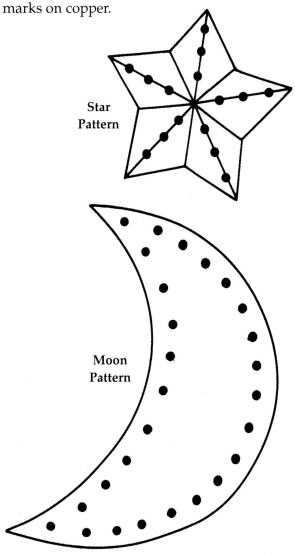

Star Pattern

Moon Pattern

Candy Canes and Lollipops

This simple swag looks delicious enough to eat!

MATERIALS

6'-long artificial pine bough swag
⅛ yard of white broadcloth
⅛ yard of red broadcloth
⅛ yard of green broadcloth
Needle and thread
1¾ yards of 14-gauge green craft wire
Wire cutters
Craft knife
Five 5½"-long, ¼"-diameter dowels
Hot glue gun and glue sticks
3⅜ yards of ³⁄₁₆"-wide red/metallic
  gold/green-striped ribbon
10 yards of 1½"-wide red ribbon
Twelve 1"-diameter red wooden beads

DIRECTIONS

1. To make one candy cane, cut one 1" x 13½" strip each from white, red and green broadcloth.

2. From craft wire, cut one 10½" length. Stack broadcloth strips, aligning ends and edges. Place one end of wire in center of stacked strips. Fold strips in half over wire; see Diagram 1. Secure strips on wire with piece of thread. Begin braiding strips around wire, compressing width of each to about ⅜"; see Diagram 2. After completing braiding to opposite end of wire, bend that end into a tight ½"-long hook. Glue in place. Remove thread. Shape cloth-covered wire into candy cane.

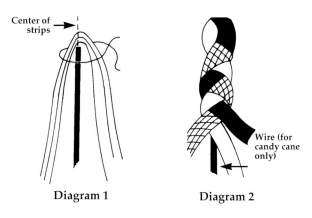

Center of strips →

Wire (for candy cane only)

Diagram 1   Diagram 2

3. Repeat to make second candy cane. Cross canes and glue together; see photo. From striped ribbon, cut one 17" length. Tie in a bow around candy canes where they cross. Trim ribbon tails diagonally.

4. Repeat to make two more pairs of candy canes. Set aside.

5. To make one lollipop, cut one 1" x 32" strip each from white, red and green broadcloth. Stack strips, aligning ends and edges. Using thread, secure lengths together at one end. Begin braiding strips together, compressing width of each to about ⅜"; see Diagram 2. Coil braided strips to make lollipop shape, gluing as needed along center of each braid; see photo. Secure ends with glue.

6. Using craft knife, sharpen one end of one dowel. Poke sharp end through edge of broadcloth lollipop at beginning of coil; see Diagram 3. Bead glue around edges of hole to secure dowel. From striped ribbon, cut one 17" length. Tie in a bow around dowel, below lollipop.

Diagram 3

7. Repeat to make four additional lollipops. Set aside.

8. To make one large bow, cut one 3¼-yard length from red ribbon. Gather center of ribbon into nine 6½"-long loops. Secure with thread ½" from bottom of loops. Fluff bow. Notch ribbon tails. Repeat to make two more large bows.

9. Glue one bow at each end of swag and one bow in middle of swag. Glue red wooden beads, candy cane pairs and lollipops to swag as desired; see photo on page 82 for ideas.

Opposite: Victorian Ribbon Star Wreath

$\mathscr{V}$ictorian Ribbon Star Wreath

As opulent as the Victorian era, this wreath may be created with ribbon colors and textures of your choice. (Project pictured on previous page.)

MATERIALS

16"-diameter straw base
10 yards of 2¾"-wide metallic gold/red
   floral ribbon; matching thread
Hot glue gun and glue sticks
9 yards of 3¼"-wide green floral wired ribbon;
   matching thread
Dressmaker's pen
Straight pins with large heads
3" length of ¼"-wide dark green
   polyester ribbon

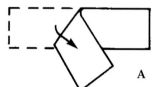 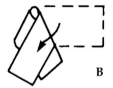

Diagram 1

Diagram 2

Diagram 3

DIRECTIONS

1. Glue one end of gold/red ribbon to back of base; allow glue to dry. Cover base by wrapping ribbon around it, overlapping wraps by about ½" and ending where wrapping began. Trim excess ribbon and reserve. Glue ribbon end to back of base.

2. To make a small ribbon star, cut six 5¼" lengths from either gold/red or green ribbon. Fold each end toward the center at an angle; see Diagram 1. Fold top section of ribbon gently back and secure with two stitches; see Diagram 2. Arrange the six folded and stitched lengths in a circle by overlapping inner points and sewing them together; see Diagram 3. To make a large ribbon star, repeat with six 8" lengths of ribbon. The model shown in the photograph has four small stars and one large star.

3. To make a small ribbon star center, cut one 20½"-long strip from either gold/red or green ribbon. Using dressmaker's pen, mark off ¼" seam allowance on each end of ribbon and 4"-long sections along one edge between seam allowances; see Diagram 4A. Sew short ends together to form circle; see Diagram 4B. Bringing edges together and matching seam with mark directly opposite, sew ribbon together; see Diagram 4C. Pinch ribbon together at remaining marks and bring to center; sew to form six loops; see Diagram 4D. Sew through middle of loops to secure star center shape. Turn loop edges under and ease fullness. Tack star center to middle of ribbon star. To make large ribbon star center, repeat with one 25½" length of ribbon and 5"-long sections.

4. Use straight pins to attach assembled ribbon stars to base, hiding pin heads in ribbon folds; see photo for placement.

5. To make hanger, make loop with polyester ribbon. Tie ends together. Glue knot to back of base at top center.

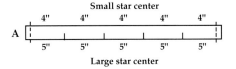

Small star center

A | 4" | 4" | 4" | 4" | 4" |

| 5" | 5" | 5" | 5" | 5" |

Large star center

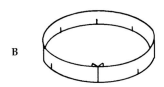

B

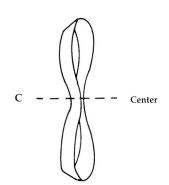

C — — | | — — Center

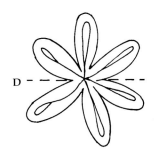

D — — ⟩ ⟨ — —

Diagram 4

*C*ountry Cottage Hearts

Perfect for holiday time or anytime, these easy fabric hearts will bring cheer to your home.

MATERIALS

Scraps of lightweight mat board
Tracing paper
Dressmaker's pen
Scraps of thirteen red, green and white
  print fabrics
⅛ yard of red/white gingham;
  matching thread
Scraps of fleece
Hot glue gun and glue sticks
Outside ring from an 8"-diameter wooden
  embroidery hoop with tension screw
3" length of ⅛"-wide polyester ribbon

DIRECTIONS

1. Trace heart pattern on page 90. From mat board, cut fourteen hearts. From fleece, cut fourteen hearts. Transfer heart pattern to wrong sides of thirteen print fabrics and one heart to wrong side of gingham, adding ½" seam allowance to each. Cut out along seam allowance. Also from gingham, cut one 4½" x 40½" piece; set aside.

2. Glue one fleece heart to each mat board heart, matching edges. Place one mat board heart fleece side down over wrong side of one fabric heart, aligning shapes. Clip fabric heart cleavage close to edge of mat board heart cleavage. Apply small amount of glue to edges of mat board. Keeping tension even, wrap seam allowance to back of mat board, clipping curves and applying additional glue as needed for smooth fit. Repeat with remaining fabric and mat board hearts.

3. Place embroidery hoop on tracing paper. Draw outline of hoop. Arrange hearts along outline right side down and with points inward, slightly overlapping widest part of hearts. Use small bead of glue to glue hearts together where they overlap, with hoop outline 1½" above points of hearts. Allow glue to set. Glue embroidery hoop to back of hearts with one heart's cleavage centered in front of tension screw; this heart becomes the top heart.

4. Fold 4½" x 40½" piece of gingham in half lengthwise with right sides together. Sew long edges together, using ¼" seam allowance; do not turn. Cut piece into one 29"-long piece, one 8½"-long piece and one 3"-long piece. Cut ends of 29" piece at a 45-degree angle. Sew across one end; turn. Slipstitch opposite end closed on 45-degree angle. Press. Turn remaining gingham pieces and press.

5. To make bow, fold 8½" gingham piece so ends match in center back. Whipstitch ends together. Place 8½" piece in center of 29" piece. Fold 3" piece in thirds and wrap snugly around center of 8½" and 29" pieces, easing fullness. Turn ends of 3" piece under; whipstitch.

6. Glue center of bow back to front of top heart's cleavage. Drape gingham tails as desired along wreath, gluing some fabric folds to backs of hearts; see photo on page 88 for ideas.

7. To make hanger, tie ends of polyester ribbon to tension screw, forming a loop.

Try This

Make a garland of fabric hearts! Make the hearts according to the directions. Cut ¾"-wide polyester ribbon to the desired length, then glue the backs of the hearts to the ribbon. Space hearts about 1½" apart.

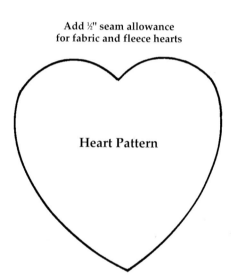

**Add ½" seam allowance
for fabric and fleece hearts**

Heart Pattern

Opposite: Paper Snowflake Choo-Choo

Paper Snowflake Choo-Choo

Look closely at this crisp snowflake to see tiny railroad cars, gingerbread men and holly leaves! (Project pictured on previous page.)

MATERIALS

Tracing paper
Pencil
One 12" x 12" piece of medium-weight
  white paper
Drafting tape
One 14" x 14" piece of mat board
Craft knife

DIRECTIONS

1. Trace snowflake pattern on pages 94 and 95. Transfer to white paper. Reverse pattern and match dots to complete snowflake shape.

2. Tape edges of paper to mat board. Using craft knife, cut out snowflake design; see diagram on page 93. It is easier to begin cutting in the center of the snowflake. Gently erase any pencil marks when cutting is complete. Mat and frame as desired.

Try This

Purchase mat board with color on both sides. Cut out two snowflakes. Coat one snowflake with spray adhesive, then glue to colored mat board. Glue second snowflake to the other side of the mat board. Punch a hole in the mat board and make a hanger from gold cord. Trim the edges of the mat board with lace or gold cord.

Make snowflakes from colored paper for a different effect. Lightly spray paint the snowflakes with metallic gold or silver paint.

Paper Snowflake Choo-Choo
Directions on page 92

■ = Areas to be cut out

Diagram

Paper Snowflake Choo-Choo
Directions on page 92

One-quarter of Snowflake Pattern
(Match dots to complete pattern)

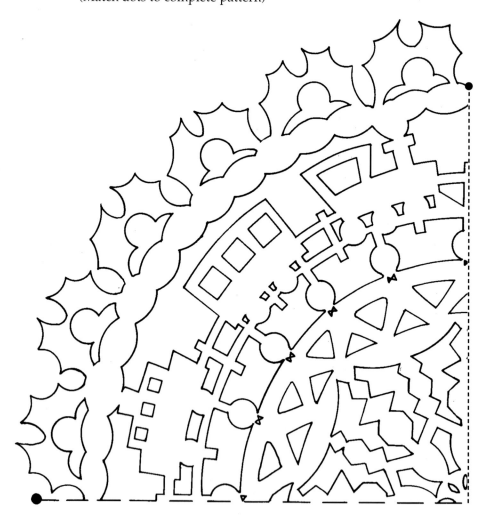

Paper Snowflake Choo-Choo
Directions on page 92

One-quarter of Snowflake Pattern
(Match dots to complete pattern)

lastic Fantasy

Yard sales and thrift stores provide the decorations for this whimsical little wreath that is as colorful as Christmas.

MATERIALS

¾ yard of 14-gauge brass wire
About seventy-five small, plastic shank
  buttons in assorted colors and shapes
1 yard of 24-gauge brass wire
⅞ yard of ⅛"-wide red ribbon

Diagram

DIRECTIONS

1. Bend 14-gauge wire around itself to form a 4"-diameter base; see diagram. Twist wire ends over completed base to secure.

2. Begin stringing buttons on 24-gauge wire. String loosely so that wire bends easily. Twist one end of wire tightly around base. Wrap base snugly with buttons on wire. Turn buttons so that some face inward and some outward, to give effect of fullness. Twist opposite end of wire tightly around base.

3. From ribbon, cut one 9" length and three 7" lengths. To make hanger, tie ends of 9" length around wire base, hiding knot under buttons. Tie 7" lengths in bows where desired on base; see photo.

Winter Redbirds and Berries

Bring warmth and color to a den or office with this elegant design.

MATERIALS

20"-diameter grapevine base
7 yards of 1½"-wide red/green plaid ribbon
Green florist's wire
Four sprigs of dried baby's breath
Green spray paint
Four sprigs of dried rose hips
Eight sprigs of red canella berries
One bunch of dried silver dollars
  (available at florist-supply stores)
Two sprigs of 18"-long preserved
  red eucalyptus
Two sprigs of 10"-long preserved
  red eucalyptus
One 5"-diameter craft bird's nest
Two red cardinal mushroom birds
Hot glue gun and glue sticks

DIRECTIONS

1. From ribbon, cut one 2½-yard length. Reserve remaining ribbon. To make bow, gather ribbon at center into sixteen 2¼"-long loops, leaving ribbon tails free. Wrap with florist's wire 1" from bottom of loops and secure, leaving wire tail. Notch ribbon tails; set aside. Glue one end of remaining ribbon to base. Wrap ribbon snugly around base; glue opposite end in place.

2. Place baby's breath on protected surface. Lightly spray with green paint. Allow to dry.

3. Glue baby's breath, rose hips, silver dollars, canella berries and eucalyptus to wreath as desired, fanning out to left and right from seven o'clock position and leaving twelve o'clock to three o'clock positions uncovered; see photo for ideas. Glue bird's nest to wreath at bottom center. Glue one bird in nest and second bird at three o'clock position; see photo. Wire bow to base below and to left of bird nest.

4. To make hanger, cut one 12" length of florist's wire. Double to make 6" length. Wrap ends around grapevine base at top back of wreath.

A Seaside Christmas

Lovely natural colors and textures combine to create a wreath with a seashore theme.

MATERIALS

10"-diameter woven pele base*
6" length of ⅛"-wide gold cord
Hot glue gun and glue sticks
Ten preserved galax leaves
Nine 2½"–3½"-diameter sand dollars
Seventy-eight assorted seashells
Seventeen sprigs of red canella berries
  (available at florist-supply stores)
Twelve assorted brass charms, such as
  Christmas trees, musical instruments
  and tiny wreaths
Six ⅜"-diameter plastic snowflakes
One small frosted pinecone
One 3"-tall cardboard Santa or other
  Christmas cutout

*See "Suppliers" on page 128.

DIRECTIONS

1. To make hanger, tie gold cord around base, making one knot close to base. Make loop and knot ends at desired length; trim excess.

2. Glue galax leaves to base, spacing evenly.

3. Glue one cluster of three sand dollars to base at top. Glue second cluster to base at middle left-hand side. Glue one sand dollar to base at middle right-hand side and two sand dollars slightly right of bottom center; see photo. Experiment with groupings of seashells and canella berries between and on top of sand dollars; see photo for ideas. Glue groupings to wreath.

4. Glue brass charms, snowflakes, pinecone and Christmas cutout to wreath as desired.

Try This

Spray paint the seashells, sand dollars and galax leaves with metallic gold or silver paint. Add clear or colored glass beads in place of the canella berries for a contemporary touch.

$\mathcal{L}$acy and Lovely Heart Wreath

Decorate your home for Christmas or add year-round beauty with this easy-to-make charmer.

MATERIALS

15"-tall heart-shaped grapevine base
Eleven 6"-diameter Battenberg lace doilies
  with scalloped edges; matching thread
Thirty-six 9"–12"-long sprigs of preserved
  green eucalyptus
Hot glue gun and glue sticks
Straight pins with large heads
7 yards of 2"-wide white, sheer ribbon
6" length of ½"-wide dark green
  polyester ribbon

DIRECTIONS

1. To make a lace flower, fold one doily in half, matching edges; see Diagram 1. Holding doily in center of fold, begin rolling loosely into a funnel shape; see Diagram 2. Sew gathering thread through completed funnel 1" above bottom; see Diagram 3. Tighten thread slightly, but do not cut. Wrap thread around funnel and secure. Arrange "petals" of flower as desired. Repeat to make ten more lace flowers. Set aside.

2. Begin gluing eucalyptus sprigs to base at bottom center, moving counterclockwise to top of right-hand lobe of heart; see photo. Glue remaining eucalyptus to base, beginning at bottom center and moving clockwise halfway up left-hand lobe; see photo.

3. Use straight pins to hold flowers in place among eucalyptus sprigs until arrangement is decided; see photo for ideas. Glue lace flowers to base. Remove pins after glue has set.

4. To make bow, cut one 1⅞-yard length from ribbon. Gather at center into fourteen 4½"-long loops. Wrap with thread 1" from bottom of loops and secure. Glue bow to wreath slightly to right of bottom center. Cut remaining ribbon into two equal lengths. Make loose knots every 7"–8" in each length. Glue one end of each length under bow. Cascade knotted ribbons around wreath as desired; see photo for ideas. Glue ends in place.

5. To make hanger, loop polyester ribbon and tie to base at back.

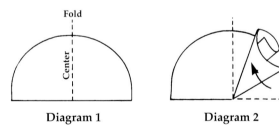

Diagram 1   Diagram 2

Diagram 3

Grand English Bow Wreath

Designed in the style of an English country house, this wreath will lend classic beauty to your home.

MATERIALS

One bundle of 8'–9'-long weeping willow
  twigs or thin grapevines
Green florist's wire
Garden clippers
One large bunch of preserved cedar sprigs
One large bunch of preserved boxwood sprigs
One large bunch of burgundy statice
Four stems of latex grape picks with leaves
Six dried lotus pods
Hot glue gun and glue sticks
Two 2'-long miniature brass coachman's horns
  (available at hobby shops)
1 yard of ⅛"-wide burgundy cord
3 yards of 1½"-wide metallic gold/
  green/red-striped ribbon

DIRECTIONS

1. Wrap center of willow twig bundle with
florist's wire to secure. Curve right half of
bundle, bringing back to center and allowing
twig ends to stick up above center 9"–10";
see Diagram 1. Secure with florist's wire.
Repeat with left half of bundle to complete
bow shape. Use gardening snips to trim
unwanted ends.

2. Layer items as follows: Glue cedar sprig
stems to center of bow shape, fanning sprigs
out to left, right and top. Glue boxwood sprig
stems to center of bow shape, fanning sprigs
out in the same manner; see photo. Cross
horns in center, with bells facing upward; see

Diagram 1

photo. Secure with glue and florist's wire. Use
wire and glue to attach crossed horns to center
of bow shape, tucking in among foliage.
Divide statice into twelve to thirteen sprigs.
Glue stems to center of bow shape among
boxwood and cedar sprigs. Glue grape pick
ends to center of bow shape with one pick
pointing upward at top, one pick at intersec-
tion of curves and one pick on either side of
downward curve; see photo. Glue lotus pod
stems to center of bow shape, placing pods
among foliage as desired.

3. To wrap horn with burgundy cord, loop
and knot one end of cord near mouthpiece;
see Diagram 2. Continue wrapping cord snugly around horn for 3½". Tuck end of cord
under last wrap; secure with glue. Repeat
with second horn.

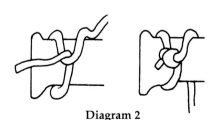

Diagram 2

4. To make bow, gather center of ribbon into nine 5"-long loops. Wrap with florist's wire about ½" above bottom of loops. Trim ribbon tails diagonally to desired length. Wire center of bow to center of crossed horns. Fluff bow and foliage to hide wire. Cascade ribbon tails to left and right sides of wreath as desired, gluing as needed to secure.

5. To make hanger, double one 14" length of florist's wire. Make loop and wrap ends around wreath at center back.

Opposite: Christmas Angel

Christmas Angel

Winter white contrasts with evergreens on this starry wreath graced with a charmingly simple needlepoint canvas angel. (Project pictured on previous page.)

MATERIALS (for angel)

½ yard of 14-count white interlock
  needlepoint canvas
Tracing paper
Dressmaker's pen
One small, round balloon
Liquid starch
Shallow pan
12" length of string
Spray bottle and water
Hot glue gun and glue sticks
Needle and white thread
12" length of ¼"-wide white lace trim
½ yard of white covered wire
¼ yard of ¼"-wide white satin ribbon
12" length of white braided wool roving
12" length of gold wire

DIRECTIONS

1. Enlarge angel skirt and cone patterns on pages 111 and 112. These patterns are printed on a grid in which each square equals 1" on the finished pattern. To enlarge patterns, use paper large enough for each finished pattern. Mark grid lines 1" apart to fill paper. Mark dots on these lines corresponding to each pattern. Connect dots. Paper with dots pre-printed at 1" intervals is available at fabric stores. A copy machine or 1" graph paper may also be used. Trace star patterns on page 110.

2. Using dressmaker's pen, transfer angel skirt, cone and star patterns to needlepoint canvas. Cut out one cone piece and four skirt pieces. Also from needlepoint canvas, cut one 7"-diameter circle for head, one 6" x 8" piece for sleeve, one 8" x 18" piece for wings and two 8" x 2½" strips for bodice. Cut out fifteen large stars, seventeen medium stars and twenty small stars; set aside.

3. Blow balloon up to 1½" diameter; tie off. Pour small amount of liquid starch into pan. Dip 7"-diameter canvas circle into starch and shape over balloon. Tie canvas edges around neck of balloon. Allow to dry overnight. Puncture balloon and remove through opening in canvas.

4. Mist cone piece lightly with water to soften. Shape cone piece so straight edges overlap ¼". Glue edges together.

5. From lace trim, cut two 6"-long pieces. Glue one to each 6" end of sleeve piece. Mist sleeve piece lightly with water. Shape into a tube, overlapping long edges ¼". Glue edges together. Cut one 16" length of covered wire. Bend 4½" of each end toward center. About ⅜" from bend at each end, twist wire firmly three times. Separate wire to make two open loops for hands. Insert wire into sleeve tube. Sew gathering thread around each sleeve near edge of lace; gather tightly around wire. Secure thread.

6. Trim excess canvas from gathered edge of head to make edge slightly wider than small end of cone. Glue head to cone. Glue center of sleeve tube to cone below head, flattening tube; see Diagram 1.

Diagram 2

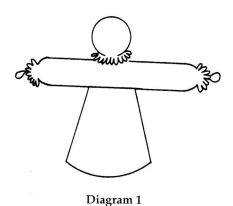

Diagram 1

7. Mist 8" x 2½" canvas strips lightly with water. Fold each strip in thirds lengthwise, accordion style, and crease. Glue edges together. Center and glue one strip to angel shoulder, wrapping each end across sleeve tube toward angel waist; glue ends behind angel. Repeat with second strip, crisscrossing first strip; see Diagram 2.

8. Make two tucks in each skirt piece according to pattern. Glue one piece to center back of angel, one piece on each side and one piece to center front, overlapping pieces as needed and allowing bottom edges of pieces to extend ½"– ¾" below bottom edge of cone. Wrap

white ribbon around angel waist, covering edges of bodice strips and skirt pieces and ending with ribbon tails in front. Tie in a bow and notch ribbon tails. Secure ribbon at back with glue, if needed.

9. Bring together short edges of wing piece, overlapping ¼". Glue edges together. Sew a gathering thread through both layers of canvas at center. Gather tightly. Secure thread. Wrap wing center tightly with covered wire. Glue wrapped center of wings to back of angel just below neck.

10. From roving, cut one 3" length; unbraid and fluff to make hair. Glue to top of head. Coil remaining roving and glue to top of head over fluffed roving for braid. To make halo, fold gold wire in half and twist tightly along entire length. Shape into a 1¾"-diameter circle, leaving a ½"-long tail. Insert end of tail into angel head at back and secure with glue.

MATERIALS (for wreath)

24"-diameter wire base
Fresh or artificial evergreen boughs
Spray bottle with water
Completed needlepoint canvas angel
Needlepoint canvas stars
3 yards of ½"-wide metallic gold ribbon
Hot glue gun and glue sticks
Heavy-weight craft wire

DIRECTIONS

1. Glue evergreen boughs to base, fanning over inside and outside edges to achieve full effect.

2. Mist angel skirt lightly with water. Shape to spread as desired over evergreen boughs at bottom center of wreath; see photo for ideas. Glue angel in place; see photo. Glue stars to wreath, with large stars along top curve, medium stars along sides and small stars at bottom on either side of angel; see photo.

3. Glue one end of gold ribbon to wreath under angel skirt. Cascade ribbon around wreath as desired, securing with glue as needed and finishing under opposite side of angel skirt; see photo for ideas.

4. To make hanger, double one 8" length of craft wire. Make loop and wrap ends around wire base at top back.

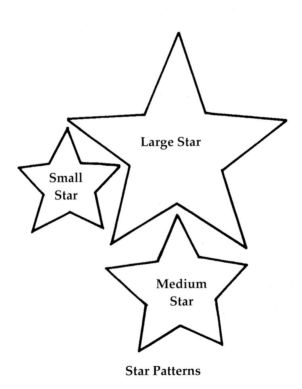

Star Patterns

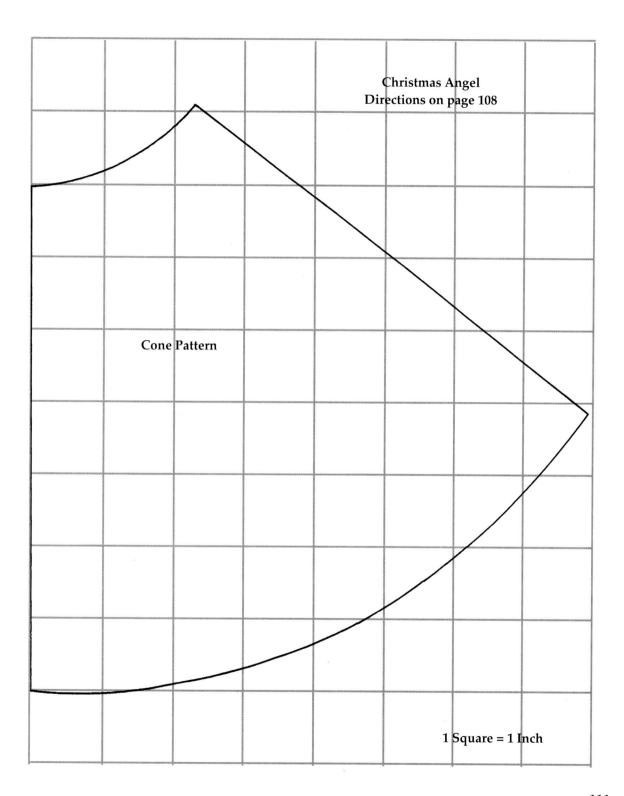

Christmas Angel
Directions on page 108

Cone Pattern

1 Square = 1 Inch

111

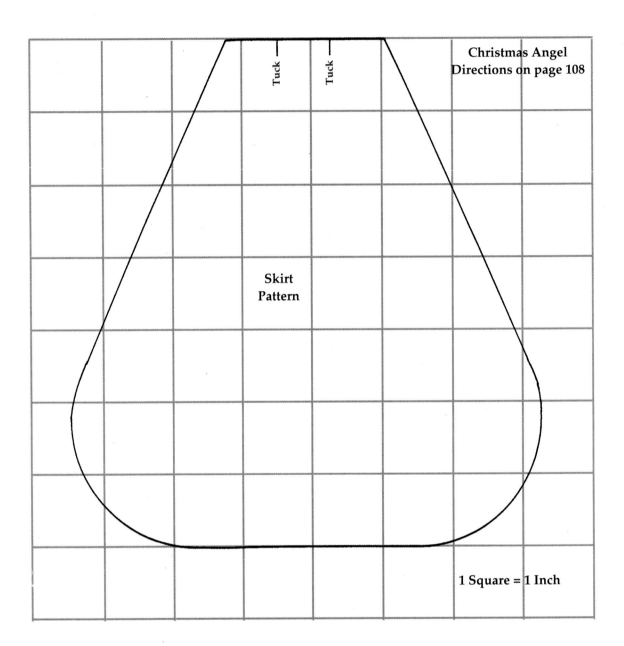

Tuck

Tuck

Christmas Angel
Directions on page 108

Skirt
Pattern

1 Square = 1 Inch

Opposite: Holiday Symphony

Holiday Symphony

Miniature instruments and sheet music suggest the traditional sounds of the season. (Project pictured on previous page.)

MATERIALS (for heart)

1⅛ cup of ground cinnamon
4 tablespoons of white glue
¾ cup of hot water
Mixing bowl
Decorative heart-shaped 4½"-tall cookie mold
Plastic straw
Cookie sheet

DIRECTIONS

1. In mixing bowl, blend glue, water and 1 cup cinnamon. Mix thoroughly by hand. Dough should be as thick as cookie dough. Sprinkle remaining cinnamon in cookie mold. Press dough into mold and allow to set for 1–2 minutes.

2. Remove cookie from mold onto wax paper by turning mold upside down and gently tapping bottom. Use straw to punch hole through cookie about ¼" below cleavage of heart.

3. Slide cookie off wax paper onto cookie sheet. Place in oven set at 150°F or warm for 2 hours. Remove to cooling rack; allow to cool.

MATERIALS (for wreath)

16"-diameter wire base
Artificial evergreen boughs with wire stems
Green florist's wire
5 yards of 5"-wide metallic gold mesh ribbon
5 yards of 1½"-wide metallic gold wired ribbon
Hot glue gun and glue sticks
Five 5"–7"-long red berry picks
18 sprigs of white statice
One 8"-long, painted miniature wooden violin with bow (available at hobby stores)
Two 6"-long, miniature decorated French horns (available at hobby stores)
Three 5"-long, decorated rolled sheet music picks (available at hobby stores)
10 yards of ½"-wide metallic gold/red braid
10 yards of ½"-wide metallic gold/green braid
10 yards of ½"-wide metallic gold/red/ green braid
Decorative heart-shaped cookie
½ yard of ⅛"-wide flat brass ribbon wire
Large felt-tip marker
Heavy-weight craft wire

DIRECTIONS

1. To make hanger, double one 8" length of craft wire. Make loop and twist ends around wire base.

2. Using florist's wire, attach evergreen boughs to base. Layer boughs, bending stems as needed for full effect.

3. To make bows, gather center of mesh ribbon into six 7"-long loops. Wrap loops tightly 1" from bottom with florist's wire, leaving about 3"-long wire tails. Gather center of wired ribbon into five 7" long loops. Wrap loops tightly ½" from bottom with florist's wire, leaving about 3"-long wire tails. Trim ribbon tails diagonally. Using wire tails, attach mesh ribbon bow to top center of wreath. Attach wired ribbon bow at center of mesh ribbon bow. Fluff bows and cascade ribbon tails as desired.

4. Divide berry picks into eight groups. Using florist's wire, attach two berry picks to wreath at center between mesh ribbon bow and wired ribbon bow. Attach remaining berry picks as desired; see photo. Secure picks with glue as needed.

5. Glue statice sprigs to wreath.

6. Using florist's wire, attach one French horn to wreath at 8 o'clock position and one at 4 o'clock position. Glue violin to wreath at bottom center with neck of violin pointing inward. Glue bow across violin strings. Glue sheet music picks to wreath at 3 o'clock, 7 o'clock and 10 o'clock positions; see photo.

7. Beginning behind bows, cascade braid around wreath, and over and under other items as desired. Secure with glue, hiding ends; see photo for ideas.

8. Cut one 8" and three 6" lengths of brass ribbon wire. Insert one end of 8" length through hole in heart-shaped cookie. Loop end and twist around itself at heart cleavage to make cookie hanger. Coil 6" lengths of brass ribbon wire, one at a time, around barrel of felt-tip marker. Remove coils from marker barrel. Twist one end of each coil around cookie hanger at heart cleavage. Twist end of hanger to base below bows to attach.

Try This

For a different look, substitute a miniature sleigh with reindeer, a snowman, angel or other Christmas figure for the violin. Replace the music picks with miniature wrapped gift packages, adding the names of family and friends to the gift tags. Replace the horns with clusters of jingle bells, cutout stars or snowflakes.

lever Candy Arch

Gumdrops and red licorice shoestrings in royal icing make a sweet fantasy arch.

MATERIALS

18"-diameter, ½"-thick flat or rounded
  Styrofoam base
Craft knife
6" length of ⅛"-wide red cord
2 cups of powdered sugar
Two egg whites
¼ teaspoon of cream of tartar
Mixing bowl
Wax paper
Spoon
1½ pounds of assorted gumdrops in
  Christmas colors and shapes
½ pound of Christmas-tree-shaped
  licorice gumdrops
Two 30"-long red licorice shoestrings

DIRECTIONS

1. Using craft knife, cut Styrofoam base horizontally in half to form arch. To make hanger, knot red cord around base at top center. Make loop with cord tails and knot ends together.

2. Make royal icing in mixing bowl by beating powdered sugar, egg whites and cream of tartar for 3–5 minutes until very thick.

3. Place base on wax paper. Working from one end to the other, spoon royal icing on top surface and edges of base and press gumdrops into icing; see photo for ideas. Use small amounts of icing as glue to layer gumdrops. Reserve small amount of icing to attach red licorice bow.

4. To make licorice bow, place licorice shoestrings side by side, matching ends. Being careful not to stretch licorice, handle both shoestrings as one and gently tie in a bow. Use reserved icing to glue knot of bow to arch near top center; see photo for placement.

Enchanted Holiday Haven

A tiny gnome peeps from the greenery and berries of this magical corner of Christmasland!

MATERIALS

24"-diameter grapevine base
One large bunch of preserved green
   eucalyptus
One large bunch of preserved cedar
One large bunch of canella berries (available
   at florist-supply stores)
Hot glue gun and glue
Two 9"-tall cardboard cones
One 7"-tall cardboard cone
Sheet moss
One nail
Green florist's wire
Two ¼"-diameter x 12"-long straight twigs
Nine ¼"-diameter x 6"-long straight twigs
One 1½"-diameter miniature straw wreath
One 4"-tall, painted plastic or wood gnome
3¼ yards of 1½"-wide metallic gold/red/
   green plaid wired ribbon
Strand of 35 miniature white Christmas lights
Heavy-weight craft wire

DIRECTIONS

1. Select area of base that will be top center of
wreath. See Placement Diagram for help with
decorating wreath. Glue seven eucalyptus
sprigs and seven or eight cedar sprigs to top
center point, pointing left. Glue five eucalyptus sprigs and eight cedar sprigs to top center
point, pointing right. Glue two or three small
eucalyptus sprigs and four or five small cedar
sprigs to top center, pointing upward.

Placement Diagram

2. Glue eucalyptus sprigs and cedar sprigs at
bottom center of base, reserving five or six
small cedar twigs. Arrange half of items to
point right and half to point left, leaving
spaces for moss trees; see Placement Diagram.
Reserve five or six small cedar sprigs.

3. To make moss trees, use nail to poke two
holes in each cardboard cone about 1" apart
and 1½" from bottom edge. Glue sheet moss
to cones, covering completely. Insert one 6"
length of florist's wire through holes in each
tree, leaving wire tails outside tree. Wire one

119

9"-tall tree to right of bottom center. Wire remaining 9"-tall tree and 7"-tall tree beside one another to left of bottom center; see photo on page 118.

4. Glue canella berry clusters to wreath at bottom center and around trees, reserving one small cluster; see photo on page 118 for ideas.

5. To make twig fence, place one 12"-long twig on work surface. Mark 6"-long twigs 1½" from each end. At first mark, glue each short twig to long twig, 1¼" apart and beginning ¼" from end of long twig; see Diagram 1A. Allow glue to set. Glue remaining 12-long twig to short twigs at second mark; see Diagram 1B.

6. Glue four reserved cedar sprigs to top center of miniature straw wreath. Glue reserved canella berries to center of sprigs. Glue straw wreath to center of top rail of twig fence. Glue remaining cedar sprigs along top rail to left and right of straw wreath. Using florist's wire, attach twig fence to back of grapevine base, so fence shows across opening above bottom center; see Placement Diagram.

7. Glue gnome to wreath among foliage at bottom center.

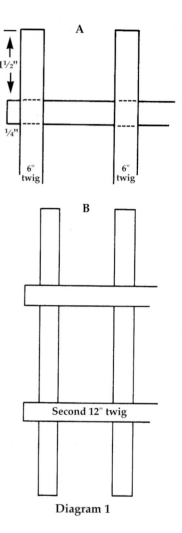

Diagram 1

8. To make bow, gather wired ribbon at center into seven 4½"-long loops and four 6½"-long loops. Wrap loops with craft wire about ½" from bottom. Cut one 6½"-long loop 1" from wire wrap to make third ribbon tail. Trim ribbon tails diagonally. Wire or glue bow to wreath at top center, covering stem ends of foliage.

9. To make hanger, double one 12" length of craft wire. Make loop and wrap ends around top center of base at back.

10. Twine string of lights through twig fence and among foliage at bottom center of wreath, leaving enough cord for plug to reach desired electrical outlet.

Cowboy Christmastime

This unique wreath is perfect for someone who loves Christmas and the Old West!
(Project pictured on previous page.)

MATERIALS

36"-diameter grapevine base
Heavyweight craft wire
10' of used barbed wire
Heavy leather gloves
Pliers
2¼ yards of 1¼"-wide green/red plaid
  wool ribbon
One large bunch of preserved juniper
  with berries
One large bunch of preserved green
  eucalyptus
One large bunch of canella berries (available
  at florist-supply stores)
Hot glue gun and glue sticks
Twenty to thirty sprigs of red statice
Fifteen 2½"-long, cylindrical wooden beads
Acrylic paints: cream, black
Paintbrush
Sixty ⅜"-diameter red wooden beads
Monofilament thread
One pair children's used cowboy boots
  (available at thrift stores or garage sales)
4' length of ¼"-wide jute rope
Three 1"-diameter silver jingle bells
3½"-long plastic or metal longhorn steer head
  (available at hobby stores or gift shops)

DIRECTIONS

1. To make hanger, fold one 30" length of
heavyweight craft wire in thirds. Make a loop
with the folded wire and wrap ends securely
around base at back. This will become the top
center of the wreath.

122

2. Wear heavy leather gloves to handle barbed
wire. To make barbed wire "bow," use pliers
to bend barbed wire into ten loops of varying
sizes, five loops on each side of center; see
Diagram 1. Leave 8"–9"-long wire tails.
Arrange loops as desired; see photo for ideas.

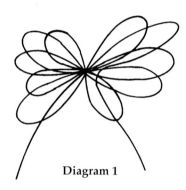

Diagram 1

3. Cut one 30" length of heavyweight craft
wire. Wrap tightly around center of barbed
wire "bow," leaving 10"–12"-long wire tails.

4. Gather wool ribbon at center into six 4½"-
long loops. Wrap loops with craft wire ½"
from bottom, leaving ribbon tails free. Trim
ribbon tails diagonally to desired length.
Position ribbon bow in center of barbed wire
"bow." Secure, using wire tails on barbed
wire "bow" and finishing with wire tails at
back of barbed wire. Set aside.

5. Beginning at top center of base, glue
about three-quarters of juniper sprigs to base,
fanning sprigs to left and right of center; see
photo. Also beginning at top center of base,

glue about three-quarters of eucalyptus sprigs to base, fanning sprigs to left and right; see photo.

6. Leaving space at top center for barbed wire and ribbon bow, glue about three-quarters of canella berries to base among foliage, fanning berries to left and right.

7. Using wire tails, attach barbed wire and ribbon bow to base in allotted space; see photo for placement.

8. Paint cylindrical wooden beads cream. Allow to dry. Paint black spots on beads to look like cow markings. Allow to dry. Cut a 2½-yard length of monofilament thread. Make a knot 8" from one end. To make garland, string four red beads, then one cylindrical bead. Repeat, alternating red beads and cylindrical beads and ending with red beads. Knot end of thread at last red bead; do not cut thread.

9. Tie one end of bead garland to base slightly left of bottom center. Loop garland along base to right of bottom center and back to center, securing loops to base as needed with additional lengths of monofilament thread; see Diagram 2. Tie opposite end of garland to base.

10. Glue remaining juniper sprigs to base, beginning about 9" to right of bottom center

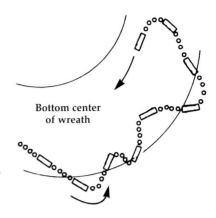

Bottom center
of wreath

Diagram 2

and fanning sprigs to left and right of starting point; see photo. Leave space for cowboy boots. Glue remaining eucalyptus to base in the same manner. Glue statice to base among foliage at bottom of base.

11. Knot both ends of jute rope. Loop rope like a lariat. Wrap one end four times around looped strands, then pass end through wrap and let hang. Set aside.

12. Glue cowboy boots together side by side, with one boot slightly ahead of other boot; see photo. Glue boots to wreath at 5 o'clock position with toes pointing left. Glue wrapped area of lariat to outside boot above heel. Glue jingle bells to wreath below outside boot's sole. Glue longhorn head to wreath near boot toes.

*H*oliday Reflections

Dress up a spare room for holiday guests!

MATERIALS

18"-diameter grapevine base with
  15"-diameter center opening
16"-diameter mirror
Heavy-weight craft wire
Fifty to sixty sprigs of preserved juniper
  with berries
Fresh evergreen boughs
Hot glue gun and glue sticks
Thirty sprigs of red canella berries
  (available at florist-supply stores)
Twenty-two to twenty-four sprigs of
  burgundy statice
6' length of silk geranium leaves
3½ yards of ½"-wide burgundy wired ribbon

DIRECTIONS

1. From craft wire, cut four 26" lengths and
one 6" length. Center mirror over center
opening of base with reflective side against
base. Crisscross 26" wire lengths over back of
mirror; see diagram. Loop and twist wire ends
tightly around thickest grapevines on base,
keeping mirror snug against base. Twist 6"
wire length around crisscrossed wires where
they cross to secure; see diagram.

2. To make hanger, double one 12" length
of wire. Make a loop and wrap ends around
base. Turn base over so reflective side of
mirror faces up.

3. Glue evergreen boughs to base. Fill in with
preserved juniper sprigs. Glue statice sprigs

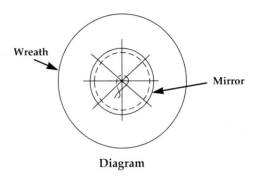

Diagram

and canella berry sprigs among foliage
as desired.

4. Twine geranium leaves around wreath over
and under other items, securing with glue as
needed.

5. From wired ribbon, cut seven 18" lengths.
Tie each length in a bow around stem of
geranium leaves length, keeping bows about
6" apart. Trim bow tails diagonally and
arrange as desired; see photo for ideas.

---

*T*ry This

Replace the mirror with an enlarged
favorite family photograph or a print of a
Christmas scene. Cut a 16"-diameter mat
board circle. Center the photograph or
print and trim it to match the mat board.
Using spray adhesive, glue the picture to
the mat board. Attach the picture to the
grapevine base as in Step 1.

$\mathcal{G}$eneral Instructions

Easy Reference Features

Materials: The Materials List identifies the items used and the quantity needed to finish the model shown in the photograph.

Directions: The directions offer step-by-step guidance for completing the model shown in the photograph, plus clear diagrams and helpful hints.

Craft Hints

Making a Grapevine Wreath Base: You will need ten 2'-5'-long grapevines, heavyweight craft wire and garden clippers. If the grapevines are not fresh, soak them in water until pliable. Choose four to six lengths. Place the vines together with ends overlapping slightly. Curve the vine lengths around to form a circle of desired diameter. Hold the vine ends together with one hand and wrap the longest vine length around the circle, catching the shorter vines. Add more vines in the same manner to achieve the desired volume. Tuck in stray ends. Secure the circle shape with craft wire as needed. Clip excess or unwanted vine pieces. Allow the wreath base to dry. Remove the craft wire before decorating the wreath.

Working with Glue: Keep a shallow dish of warm water and a clean cloth handy. Dip your fingers in the water and dry them on a cloth to remove glue before handling materials.

To control overspray when using spray adhesive or spray paint, cover the work surface with newspapers. Replace sticky newspapers before spraying the next item. Keep sprays away from hot glue gun or open flame.

Drying Fruits: Cut citrus fruits into ¼"-thick slices. Cut apples into ⅛"-thick slices and remove seeds. To retain the bright color, dip each slice into liquid fruit preservative (available at supermarkets). Place slices 1" apart on a cooling rack. Place the rack on a cookie sheet. Leave it overnight in oven set at 150°F or warm. Whole pomegranates, which have a more porous interior, may be dried in the same manner. Large whole fruits with dense, solid centers, such as oranges or apples, do not dry well.

Drying Flowers, Seed Pods and Foliage: Since fragile items can break during drying, first spray each item liberally with a fixative, such as hair spray.

Air-dry items by hanging them upside down in loose bunches of six to ten stems. Hang in a spare room, garage or shed.

Quick-acting, moisture-absorbing silica gel crystals can also be used (available at craft-supply stores). Pour a 1"-thick layer of crystals into a metal, glass or plastic container. Place the items on top with adequate space between each. Cover them with more crystals. Add another layer of items and then more crystals until the container is full. Check the items every other day. When dry, remove them from the container and use a small, dry paintbrush to whisk away the crystals.

Working with Dried Materials: Keep a tea kettle or pan of water on a hot plate or warm stove burner in work area. Hold dried roses in the steam for a few seconds, then blow into the blossoms. The roses will open. Shape the petals with your fingers.

Recondition most dried flowers by slightly moistening them with water from a spray bottle or by holding them in steam like roses. Do this just before attaching the flowers to the wreath.

Dyed and/or preserved foliage should not be placed in areas of high humidity or in damp outdoor weather. It might absorb enough moisture to drip, causing the dye to run.

When using hot glue to attach pod stems, pinecones or hard, glossy items to a wreath, first lightly scrape or sand the surface to be glued.

Spray dried items with a light coating of a sealer such as Floralife Dri-Seal (available at florist-supply stores). This will protect the natural beauty of the items. Always keep dried items away from heat sources or open flame.

Storing Dried Materials: Keep unused dried flowers and foliage in plastic bags. This prevents them from becoming too dry and brittle.

Working with Paper Ribbon: Natural paper ribbon is tightly wound. Soak it in water before untwisting it. Colored paper ribbon is wound more loosely and does not require soaking. Paper ribbon can be untwisted to 2"–6" widths, as desired. See individual project directions for the required paper ribbon width.

Making Tassels: Wind ribbon, yarn, floss or other fiber around cardboard triangle as many times as desired; see Diagram A. Secure bundle with strand of fiber; see Diagram B. Cut wound strands opposite tie; see Diagram C. Tightly wrap a single strand around bundle about one-third of the way down; see Diagram D. Tie ends. Push ends into tassel to hide them. Trim tassel to desired length.

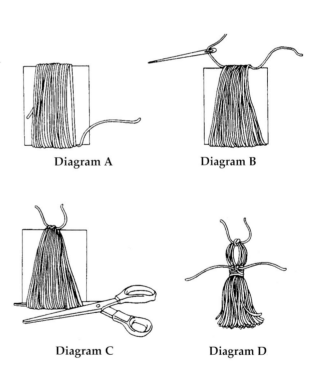

Diagram A   Diagram B

Diagram C   Diagram D

uppliers

For a merchant near you, write to one of the suppliers below.

Acrylic paints
Pearlescent acrylic paint
Delta Technical Coatings, Inc.
2550 Pellissier Place
Whittier, CA 90601

Seed beads
Mill Hill division of
Gay Bowles Sales, Inc.
P.O. Box 1060
Janesville, WI 53547

Dried pele base
Coast Wholesale Dry Flowers & Baskets
149 Morris Street
San Francisco, CA 94107

Glue
Aleene's
A Division of Artis, Inc.
85 Industrial Way
Buellton, CA 93427

Ribbons
C. M. Offray and Son, Inc.
Route 24, Box 601
Chester, NJ 07930